tree-spotting

tree-spotting

A Simple Guide to Britain's Trees

Ros & Nell Bennett

WELBECK

Published by Welbeck
An imprint of Welbeck Non-Fiction Limited
Part of Welbeck Publishing Group
Based in London and Sydney
www.welbeckpublishing.com

First published by Welbeck in 2022

A CIP catalogue record for this book is available from the British Library

ISBN
Hardback – 978-1-78739-870-2

Typeset by Envy Design Ltd
Printed in the UK by CPI Group (UK) Ltd, Croydon CRO 4YY

10 9 8 7 6 5 4 3 2 1

To John

Nell (your illustrator) and Ros (your narrator) in the Apennines, Italy, in the summer of 1990 while Ros was leading a botany course.

Contents

Meet my Mother
by Nell

BEFORE I COULD walk, Mum (Ros) strapped me to her back and took me all over Europe. While she taught enthusiastic naturalists in her open-air classrooms, my baby bouncer would be hung from a suitable tree branch, and I would be entertained by glorious wilderness and local butterflies. My childhood was a constant adventure, where valuing and respecting nature was encouraged at every opportunity.

Even today, with specimens under one arm and maps and books under the other, Mum can be found anywhere from the classrooms of Cambridge to the Cork Oak forests of Córdoba. For 50 years, this incredible botanist has been teaching and inspiring thousands of people with her deep love and knowledge of botany. Mum will now be your guide, helping you learn and identify the exquisite trees that surround you.

Tree-spotting

My hugely unique childhood felt (almost) normal to me, but was a great source of amusement to my friends. It was not uncommon to open the fridge and find bundles of twigs awaiting identification or a tray of seeds to be sorted, rather than tasty morsels to be snuck. Parties were preceded by feverish activity, involving the whole family having to roll up their sleeves and scrump apples for curried apple soup (a rather interesting vegan dish) or gather elderflowers to ferment in lemon and sugar to make elderflower champagne. This sublime concoction smells of summer and leaves all guests blissfully intoxicated. Our family recipe has been perfected over many years. Initial experiments were not so sublime: I have an early memory of bottles exploding like cannons, leaving a sticky goo all over the pantry. Christmas presents are in the same spirit – the overzealous quince tree nearly collapsed with so much fruit one year that our extended family received quince jelly, quince marmalade and quince gin three years in a row.

It would not surprise you that my parents' garden is wild and bursting with birds, insects, toads and (mostly native) trees. Traditional fruit trees are my favourite addition. There are cherry trees whose incandescent blossom covers the ground like snow each spring. There is an ancient-looking mulberry, with gnarled and wizened boughs bearing bulging berries ideal for infusing in liquor or making vermilion crumble. The prize is our walnut tree. In early summer my father can be seen gathering green walnuts ready for pickling, determined to get in before the ambitious squirrels.

As a botanist, my mother can, apparently, identify any plant in the British countryside that you might stumble across.

Over the years she has shared her knowledge with a staggering 10,000+ people. Naturalists from all over the world come to be inspired and guided by her, and some return frequently to study different plant groups. Having been a bystander myself on many of these courses, I see why: her patient passion. A session with Mum forges ahead into the forest, whatever the weather. Immediately, she will show the group how to identify the nearest tree. She breaks down the complex dimensions of botany for all to understand and to revel in wonder at nature's purest building blocks. She always exclaims at how exquisite every plant looks, and you have to agree – even when it, and all of us, are standing in the pouring rain. Her love and knowledge of the botanical world is utterly infectious.

While she did not ignite the scientist within me, she did kindle an everlasting love and curiosity for the beauty of the natural world. While she taught, I would endlessly draw and paint flowers, seeds and butterflies. Amazingly, my rigorously scientific mother found countless ways to nourish my creative streak, while instilling in me much of her floral knowledge. We gathered Beech, Sycamore and lime leaves, and placed them on photo paper to make splendid silhouettes. We made Andy Goldsworthy-like sculptures from autumnal maple leaves, and sundials from twigs. We made glockenspiels from laurel logs and played 'Clair de lune'. When a storm floored our Weeping Willow, we wove baskets from the whip-like branches. We set seeds in plaster and carved abstract forest ferns into clay. With each creative expedition, she subtly told me what each tree was and in what way these leaves or that bud were unique.

Our house is home to an enviable library holding countless

identification, ecological and historical books on the flora and fauna of the world. As my love of art grew, my father expanded the art section, encouraging me with titles like Brian Cook's Batsford books on rural Britain, which use a counter-intuitive palette to depict striking pink and lilac conifers. John Nash's surreal country scenes, showing pockets of forest between raucous golden fields, added more depth and dimension. Black and white woodcuts of hedgerows by the likes of Charles William Taylor were well thumbed. Encyclopaedic tomes with botanically precise illustrations of catkins and leaves, drawn by Stella Ross-Craig, provided a contrasting perspective. Little did I know at the time that I would one day reference these books, and that they would continue to inspire me as I illustrate a book that my mother would write.

In my mind the botanist and illustrator Camillo Karl Schneider could not have put it better: '… in descriptive botany the image must always be predominant to the word. It is of greatest importance to fix the recognized matter in the picture. When comparing sketches, differences, which can only be discerned with difficulty from the description, often become strikingly obvious.'[1]

We hope that our insatiable passion for nature, mixed with Mum's boundless knowledge of trees, and my endless desire to draw, will make this book a glorious way for you to learn and identify trees in the UK. I now live in Singapore, surrounded by trees and plants that look nothing like those you are about to see in this guide, but that are equally as exquisite and intriguing. To illustrate this book while far from

1 Camillo Karl Schneider, Dendrologische Winterstudien (Gustav Fischer, 1903). Translated into English by Bernd Schultz, *Identification of Trees and Shrubs in Winter* (Kew Publishing, 2018).

home during the pandemic has been a wonderful, if slightly homesick-inducing, journey! I can't wait until our next walk together in the Singapore Botanic Gardens, where Mum can quench my curiosity and tell me how epiphytes function, or why that fern is integral to this woodland ecosystem.

I know that this book will also quench your thirst. You will find her knowledge fascinating, and her methods for identifying the 52 native trees of Britain engaging and simple. I hope that each walk will now be filled with a new level of wonder and adoration for these bodacious British trees.

Nell Bennett

Introduction

TREES HAVE PLAYED a vital role throughout human history. We have relied on trees for berries and nuts; for shelter and clothing; for tools and fuel; for the wheels of transport and the wheels that generated power. They have formed the framework of our warships and the massive roofs of our great cathedrals. Trees are the source of life-changing medicines and life-enhancing beverages. They have provided materials that have lasted hundreds of years and others that are as ephemeral as a match. What is less obvious, and even more important, is that trees helped form our atmosphere and continue to clean and enrich the air we breathe.

Despite all this, our lifestyles today mean that most people no longer 'know' trees. This book hopes to address that by helping you get to know them by name, but in order to understand them better, it is also an introduction to the social life of trees – their family relationships, how they reproduce, defend themselves, and interact with each other and with other living things. We also cover their history in Britain. For what's in a name if we don't get to know them better and see how they fit into society – into the ecosystem of life?

So we'll begin with an introduction to the main 'characters' – those trees that some readers will recognise as familiar. We then move on to discuss what makes trees tick, before coming to the section in the book that deals with naming trees. Here we help you learn how to look at trees – what to look for that will give you clues to their identity.

Although there are many trees that you quickly learn to recognise, there are others where you need to play detective and look for key identification features. We have constructed some simple-to-use keys to help guide you. We hope you will find this section useful and fun. Here we encourage you to look closely, especially at the leaves and buds. This will give you a new perspective on the beauty of each tree as you become more intimately acquainted with it.

We strongly recommend that you acquire a hand lens (magnification of 10x). Looking at trees through a lens opens up another world of wonder. (NB a regular magnifying glass won't do – it's not strong enough.)

Finally, we devote a couple of pages to each tree, focusing on its identification features, its habitat and its natural distribution in Britain. We also consider a few of the ways that wildlife and mankind rely on trees. Each species has its own story to tell and once you have its name, you have the key to unlock the door to much more information.

Some of the trees we cover could equally be referred to

as shrubs. Essentially, a tree has a single trunk and tends to grow tall, while shrubs are multitrunked and generally lower-growing. But where to draw the line? Botanists don't. But we have made the arbitrary decision to include all trees and shrubs that typically exceed 4 metres in height if given the opportunity to do so.

There are over 1,500 different species of trees found in the British Isles. To cover all of them would be overwhelming in a book of this type. We narrowed it down to 52 species, 43 of which are native to these islands, and the remaining 9 of which are 'honorary' natives, brought here long ago by early humans. You are most likely to find native trees in semi-natural woodlands and in the hedgerows of rural places. Many of them will also occur in parks and gardens alongside exotic species. We have omitted trees more recently introduced from foreign parts.

Fifty-two is considerably less daunting than 1,500, but even so, one is tempted, at first glance, to judge that they all look alike. Let *Tree-spotting* help you – first, by agreeing that yes, some *do* look alike. This is because they arc related to each other – they share family characteristics. In *Tree-spotting*, we discuss them in their family groups, which makes the task seem less daunting. It also means that you have a framework for identifying the other 1,448 exotic species, for many of these will fit into one or another of the family boxes. But don't let's get carried away. Let's meet some of the main characters first.

FEATURES OF THE BOOK

There are many features in this book, in addition to the text, to help you understand and identify trees.

Nell's illustrations of leaves, buds, twigs and fruits highlight important features of each tree species.

Accompanying the species drawings are useful distribution maps, giving you an insight into where each species grows. Black indicates native distribution; grey indicates where it has been introduced. We are indebted to the BSBI for permitting us to modify their distribution maps.

You will see vertical lines next to many of the drawn features. This is a measurement scale to indicate the size of the specimen in life. The line always represents 1cm. There is also a centimetre rule on page 304.

Gender symbols also accompany some of the flower drawings, to signify if the specimen is female♀, male ♂or hermaphrodite ♀.

Also adjacent to many flower illustrations is a summary of the floral features – a floral formula (p. 291).

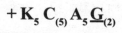

$$+ K_5\, C_{(5)}\, A_5\, \underline{G}_{(2)}$$

ABBREVIATIONS

Here are some common abbreviations that will be used throughout the book. You will soon become familiar with them.

AM	arbuscular mycorrhiza
APG	Angiosperm Phylogeny Group
BP	Before Present
BSBI	Botanical Society of Britain and Ireland
COP	United Nations Climate Change Conference ('Conference of the Parties')
DED	Dutch elm disease
EcM	ectomycorrhiza
ID	identification
KCAG	shorthand used in floral formulae (p. 291) (K = calyx, C = corolla, A = androecium and G = gynoecium)
mya	millions of years ago
ssp	subspecies
<	less than
>	more than
(4)	occasionally as great as number indicated
~	approximately

PART ONE

GETTING TO KNOW BRITAIN'S TREES

1

Britain's Most Familiar Trees

D O YOU EVER find, when reading a novel, that you
reach Chapter 4 and realise that you can't remember
who is who? This book is not a novel, but it has characters –
52 of them, and I'm going to make some brief introductions
in this first chapter. But don't worry – you will find them
summarised later, listed in their family groups. When people
come to me saying they can't tell one tree from another and
asking if I can help, I start by asking them to list those they do
know. It is surprising how long that list can be. Try it. Some
readers will already be familiar with several trees – often
more than they realise. Others are entering a whole new and
fascinating world. Let's start with the most familiar.

OAK

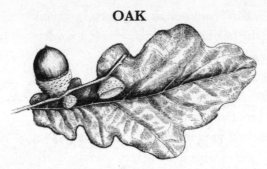

The oak tree is embedded firmly in British culture. A mature tree can be massive and is the tree that would, if we let it, naturally dominate much of our countryside, as it once did. Both its leaves and its nuts (acorns) are used to symbolise power, authority or victory. We say, 'Mighty oaks from little acorns grow.' They occur sculpted on architectural features. They have significance in heraldic arms and have been adopted as an emblem by the National Trust. The acorn and the shape of the leaves are iconic. Most people would be able to recognise an oak if they found a live specimen.

There are over 500 different species (types) of oak in the world, eight of which grow in Britain, but only two of which are native – Pedunculate Oak and Sessile Oak. In this book we will focus on our native species and we'll discuss what is meant by 'native' as far as trees are concerned. The scientific name given to all oaks is *Quercus* and you can specify each species of oak by adding a specific epithet. *Quercus robur* is Pedunculate Oak and *Quercus petraea* is Sessile Oak.

Common names for species with a wide distribution vary from country to country, but scientific names are internationally accepted which certainly helps with communication for anyone who is prepared to use the scientific names. In this book we will use common names, but you can find the scientific names in the heading for each of the species descriptions.

HOLLY

Another very familiar tree is one that we associate strongly with Christmas festivities. It also has iconic features – red berries and evergreen leaves with spiky margins. Holly, of course. There is only one holly, or *Ilex*, in Britain and Europe – *Ilex aquifolium*. But there are 479 more species globally.

CONIFERS

'Christmas trees' belong to a distinct group of predominantly evergreen trees whose leaves are needle-shaped and whose 'fruits' are almost always cones – the conifers. Several different species are used to decorate our homes at Christmastime. The current favourite is Nordmann Fir (also known as Caucasian Fir) because it is least likely to litter the sitting room floor with needles. A Norway Spruce stands in Trafalgar Square each year. Many species of foreign conifers are grown in parks and gardens and in forestry plantations, but only three are native to the British Isles, the most common of which is Scots Pine, *Pinus sylvestris*.

CHERRIES

Wild cherries put on fabulous displays of white blossom in April to June. We have two native species of cherry – Wild Cherry, *Prunus avium* and Bird Cherry, *P. padus*. And they have a close relative, Blackthorn, *P. spinosa*, which, you've guessed it, has very spiny twigs. Blackthorn is commonly found in hedgerows and, sometimes as early as February, it becomes a mass of flowers before the leaves burst.

The fruits of cherries need no description, but they are eagerly devoured by thrushes and other birds so, if you blink, you'll miss them in the wild. Blackthorn fruits are called sloes. They look like small plums and have a stone-like protection around the seed like cherries. But sloes are so bitter that they suck the moisture out of your mouth, particularly if they are eaten before they are absolutely ripe. They are best mixed with sugar and steeped in gin.

There are other blossom-bearing trees like the cherries and each of their flowers are similar in structure to a small single rose flower with five petals, i.e. not like the cultivated (and sterile) double roses which are a mass of petals and much loved by gardeners.

All trees and herbaceous plants that have a rose-type flower belong to the Rose family – the Rosaceae (pronounced 'rose-A-C'). The flowers of members of the Rosaceae are unusual in having numerous (more than 15) stamens, the pollen-producing organs. These are an obvious feature to spot, if you look closely – lots of pin-like structures.

Those of you who have already enjoyed close inspection of such blossoms may well be familiar with other members of this family. They all have succulent fruits that look similar to, but are in fact different from, those of *Prunus*. Those that are native to Britain include two species of hawthorn, or *Crataegus*; Crab Apple or *Malus sylvestris*; and three species of the genus *Sorbus* – Whitebeam, *S. aria*; Wild Service Tree, *S. torminalis*; and Rowan, *S. aucuparia*.

BIRCHES

Many people are familiar with the 'silver' trunk of the Silver Birch, *Betula pendula*. The trunks of mature trees are not silver, but white (with broad, vertical black cracks) and shine out among the sombre brown trunks of other trees. Notice that the scientific name alludes to another characteristic feature – its graceful, fine and pendulous branches.

MAPLES

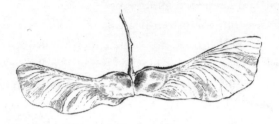

You may have heard about, or – better still – seen the wonderful autumn colours of the various maple species that swathe much of the eastern fringes of northern America. The generic name for the maples is *Acer*, and we have just one native species – Field Maple, *Acer campestre*. It has the same basic maple-shaped leaf and the characteristic helicopter-type fruits shared by all maples.

The maples used to be the sole members of their family, the Aceraceae, which was considered a sister family to the tropical soapberry family, called the Sapindaceae. Recent genetic research has demonstrated that the relationship is closer than was previously recognised and they should all be regarded as part of the same family – the Sapindaceae.

WILLOWS

Weeping Willow is a species that many people feel able to pick out from a line-up of different trees. Its graceful, weeping habit and long thin leaves are unmistakable. Globally, there are 400 species of willows, *Salix*. The genus is also very well represented in Britain, with over 20 species. But most of them do not have long thin leaves and only Weeping Willow has

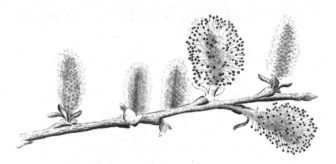

pendulous, weeping branches. So, how can you spot a willow? What do they have in common? Plenty. But for starters, most are rooted in wet ground and all bear catkins that develop into short spikes of tiny capsules; these burst open to release thousands of minute plumed seeds that disperse in the wind or simply drift on air currents.

Poplars, *Populus,* share these characteristics but differ in subtle ways that will have more significance later in the book. Poplars and willows share enough features to warrant grouping them together into a family – the Salicaceae (named after the genus *Salix*, willows).

TREE SPECIES AND THEIR FAMILIES

The Family Matching Game on page 33 includes the more familiar trees of those that we will be discussing in this book. Some of them belong to one of the families that we have already considered in this chapter. Others do not.

See if you can match them up before looking at the family groups on the next page.

This is a conversation I often have, especially with my beginner groups. It helps them acknowledge that they often know more about the trees around them than they believed. If you are a true beginner and are really not at all familiar with any more trees – see if you can find clues hidden in their names, both common and scientific.

Before you begin, consider this list of some tree families, including those you have just read about.

Common name	Scientific name
Holly family	*Aquifoliaceae*
Birch family	*Betulaceae*
Dogwood family	*Cornaceae*
Oak family	*Fagaceae*
Pine family	*Pinaceae*
Buckthorn family	*Rhamnaceae*
Rose family	*Rosaceae*
Willow family	*Salicaceae*
Soapberry family	*Sapindaceae*
Elm family	*Ulmaceae*

The Family Matching Game

Here is a list of some tree species. See if you can work out which family they belong to from the list above. (Note that scientific names for species will always appear in italics.)

Common name	Scientific name	Write the family name in this column
Alder Buckthorn	*Frangula alnus*	
Aspen	*Populus tremula*	
Beech	*Fagus sylvatica*	
Buckthorn	*Rhamnus cathartica*	
Crab Apple	*Malus sylvestris*	
Dogwood	*Cornus sanguinea*	
Downy Birch	*Betula pubescens*	
Osier	*Salix viminalis*	
Scots Pine	*Pinus sylvestris*	
Small-leaved Elm	*Ulmus minor*	
Sycamore	*Acer pseudoplatanus*	
Wych Elm	*Ulmus glabra*	

Find the answers on the next page.

Britain's Native and Honorary Native Trees in Family Order

Key:
FAMILY (Order)
Common name *Scientific name*

* denotes the non-native species.

PINACEAE (Pinales)
Scots Pine *Pinus sylvestris*

TAXACEAE (Pinales)
Yew *Taxus baccata*

CUPRESSACEAE (Pinales)
Juniper *Juniperus communis*

BUXACEAE (Buxales)
Box *Buxus sempervirens*

CELASTRACEAE (Celastrales)
Spindle *Euonymus europaeus*

SALICACEAE (Malpighiales)
Aspen *Populus tremula*
Black Poplar *Populus nigra*
Bay Willow *Salix pentandra*
*Crack Willow *Salix x fragilis*
*White Willow *Salix alba*
*Almond Willow *Salix triandra*
Purple Willow *Salix purpurea*
*Osier *Salix viminalis*
Goat Willow *Salix caprea*
Grey Willow *Salix cinerea*

ULMACEAE (Rosales)
Wych Elm *Ulmus glabra*
*English Elm *Ulmus procera*
*Field Elm *Ulmus minor*

FAGACEAE (Fagales)
Beech *Fagus sylvatica*
*Sweet Chestnut *Castanea sativa*
Sessile Oak *Quercus petraea*
Pedunculate Oak *Quercus robur*

BETULACEAE (Fagales)
Silver Birch *Betula pendula*
Downy Birch *Betula pubescens*
Alder *Alnus glutinosa*
Hazel *Corylus avellana*
Hornbeam *Carpinus betulus*

SAPINDACEAE (Sapindales)
Field Maple *Acer campestre*
*Sycamore *Acer pseudoplatanus*

MALVACEAE (Malvales)
Large-leaved Lime *Tilia platyphyllos*
*Lime *Tilia x europaea*
Small-leaved Lime *Tilia cordata*

ROSACEAE (Rosales)
Blackthorn *Prunus spinosa*
Wild Cherry *Prunus avium*
Bird Cherry *Prunus padus*
Crab Apple *Malus sylvestris*
Hawthorn *Crataegus monogyna*
Midland Hawthorn *Crataegus
                          laevigata*
Rowan *Sorbus aucuparia*
Whitebeam *Sorbus aria*
Wild Service Tree *Sorbus torminalis*

RHAMNACEAE (Rosales)
Buckthorn *Rhamnus cathartica*
Alder Buckthorn *Frangula alnus*

ELAEAGNACEAE (Rosales)
Sea Buckthorn *Hippophae rhamnoides*

CORNACEAE (Cornales)
Dogwood *Cornus sanguinea*

ERICACEAE (Ericales)
Strawberry Tree *Arbutus unedo*

OLEACEAE (Lamiales)
Wild Privet *Ligustrum vulgare*
Ash *Fraxinus excelsior*

AQUIFOLIACEAE (Aquifoliales)
Holly *Ilex aquifolium*

VIBURNACEAE (Dipsacales)
Elder *Sambucus nigra*
Guelder-rose *Viburnum opulus*
Wayfaring Tree *Viburnum lantana*

Grouping the trees into genera and families of lookalikes in this way is not just simply fulfilling a need for orderliness. These are much more than just lookalike groups – they are genetically related. Species within a genus are genetically very similar and are consequently believed to share a common ancestor. Similarly, genera within a family are also genetically related, although through a more ancient ancestor. A group of related families is called an 'order' – see the table above where the order names finish with '–ales', e.g. Rosales. Our trees are just a small representation of all the seed plants in the world. There are over 300,000 species and they are generally believed to have evolved from a single ancestral type. These 300,000 species are grouped into over 13,000 genera, 428 families and 70 orders. In this wider context you can see the value of orders.

So, we have classified trees into groups. The study of classification is called taxonomy. Nowadays, taxonomists rely primarily on genetic research to help them organise the classification system. The current system and the one used here is referred to as the APG (Angiosperm Phylogeny Group) system. Inevitably, in light of recent genetic research, APG found it necessary to impose a little reorganising of the older system. But the early botanists, seeking a similar classification – i.e. based on relationships, but using different criteria such as floral structure and constituent chemistry – got it largely right.

Genes don't just determine appearances. Closely related species will share a chemistry and may react similarly to environmental conditions. They tend to reproduce in similar ways and in some cases may be able to interbreed to produce hybrids.

This demonstrates the fundamental value of understanding the taxonomy of plants. If the timber of one member of a family is rot resistant, the timber of other species in that same family may also be. If one species produces therapeutic volatile oils, other members of the same family might do the same. Of course, there are exceptions and each species will behave slightly differently from the others in its family. When I come across a new species and am unfamiliar with its name, my first question is: 'What family does it belong to?' That way, I instantly have an insight into what makes the plant tick.

The following chapters focus on different aspects of what makes a tree tick. I urge you to read them wearing a taxonomist's hat.

2

Blossoms and Berries

FLOWERS

FLOWERS DON'T FEATURE strongly in this book because they are flecting and usually out of reach. But they are fundamental to the production of fruit and seeds and hence to the continuation of the species. And what's more, they are exquisitely beautiful.

When we think of flowers, we automatically think of their showy petals. But these are of secondary importance to the other parts of the flower – the reproductive organs. These are the male stamens, which produce pollen grains that contain the male gametes, and the female gynoecium. The latter is made up of two carpels (tiny bags that are either fused together or free from each other) that contain one or more ovules, which contain the female gametes. Ovules develop into seeds once the male and female gametes combine to create a new embryo.

Flower Anatomy

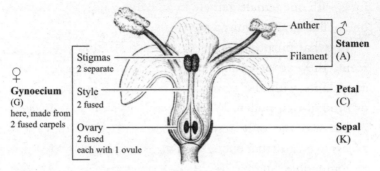

For the male gamete to reach the female, pollen grains must first travel from a ripe anther – the topmost portion of the stamen – to the receptive tip (stigma) of a carpel. This is typically achieved by hitching a ride on an insect foraging for the nectar produced at the base of the flower. This transfer of pollen can occur between anthers and stigmas of the same or different flowers on the same plant – in which case, it is self-pollination and effectively inbreeding – or between anthers and stigmas of flowers borne on different plants. So long as the pollen and ovules are from compatible individuals, i.e. generally of the same species, it is cross-pollination and considered genetically a better option. (Of course, pollination can occur between totally different and incompatible species, such as between a lime and a cherry, in which case, pollination is invalid and no fertilisation will happen.)[2] Compatibility is determined by the stigma. A compatible pollen grain is permitted to grow a pollen tube down the inside of the style. The male gamete migrates

---

2 Sometimes fertilisation can occur between different (normally closely related) species, resulting in a hybrid that is usually infertile.

down the pollen tube into the ovary at the bottom, where it fuses with one female gamete in an ovule – note that there is one pollen grain required per ovule.

So what purpose do the petals serve? Using colour and scent, they attract pollinating insects that associate these attractants with the reward of sweet, high-energy nectar or protein-rich pollen. When flowering plants first evolved, pollen was the only reward and had to be produced in excess to ensure that enough survived predation and reached a compatible stigma. This was expensive and wasteful for the plant, so an alternative lure to potential pollinators evolved – nectar.

Apple and cherry blossom is very conspicuous – the flowers are large, with bright white petals that contrast clearly with the background green. They produce nectar and pollen in excess (note the abundance of stamens, which is a feature of this family – Rosaceae). By contrast, the flowers of Spindle are much smaller and a creamy green – not nearly so showy. To compensate for this, they are clustered together, so that collectively they make a stronger impact. The precise arrangement of flowers in their clusters is also a consistent characteristic of each species in Rosaceae. For instance, the stalks of Wild Cherry flowers all arise from the same point, so they hang in lose cluster referred to as an umbel, while those of Bird Cherry are borne in a raceme – with their individual stalks attached spirally along a common central stem. These different types of arrangements are referred to as inflorescences.

We learn to recognise many flowers by familiarity. But more often, we need to look closely to check for distinguishing features. For example, Buckthorn has four petals while Alder Buckthorn has five. Midland Hawthorn has two carpels making up its gynoecium, while Hawthorn has only one, as is reflected in the number of styles. Close observation not only confirms identity, but it also comes with its own rewards – the intricate detail of floral design is one of nature's marvels. Seen through a hand lens, one enters another beautiful and awe-inspiring world.

The flower structure of each species is often unique and can be summarised in a shorthand floral formula. We have used floral formulae in this book to save space. They are easy to interpret. (See page 291.)

Flowering plants evolved in tropical environments, where there are few limitations to growth – plenty of water, continual warmth and diverse and abundant insects to assist with pollination.[3] The greatest challenge is competition for light. Trees fare well but most have to be shade-tolerant as youngsters. Herbaceous plants struggle on the forest floor unless they can tolerate the half-light. Some twine their way up to the light or others, known as epiphytes, find niches on the higher trunks and branches of the trees.

An alternative strategy is to escape the rat race of the jungle and exploit more open, sunny habitats of higher altitudes or latitudes. Here, plants are exposed to generally drier climates, where temperatures are more extreme and exacerbated by wind. These climatic extremes increase towards the tops of high mountains and towards the poles, and

---

3   In the tropics, in addition to insects, certain birds and bats are specialised to share the role of pollinator. Even in Britain incidental pollination is effected by, for example, Blue Tits foraging for insects among the flowers and . See also p. 178.

the diversity of pollinating insects dramatically decreases. The plant communities of these higher altitudes and latitudes rely less and less on insects for pollination and more and more on the wind, which is plentiful but has little regard for attractive blossoms. For those species that have abandoned entomophily (insect pollination) and embraced anemophily (wind pollination), large showy petals are not only redundant but also a hindrance to the passage of the wind. The production of nectar to attract insects becomes a waste of energy. But once again, pollen must be produced copiously because the wind is a haphazard transporting agent and most will never land on a stigma, compatible or otherwise. Anemophilous pollen grains are even smaller and more featureless compared to insect-borne pollen. They have no need for a surface 'sticky' with miniscule projections to catch on the bodies of insects.

In temperate regions of the world, more than half of the plants rely on wind pollination. Notable among these are the grasses, sedges, rushes and all of the more widespread and dominant trees, such as oak, birch, hazel and pine. Most anemophilous trees flower before the leaves burst and get in the way of the wind. Their flowers are small and unisexual, either male or female. The male flowers of most species are borne in catkins consisting of hundreds of individual flowers; these are usually arranged in a tight spiral around long flexible stems that shake in the wind. Each flower consists of little more than a bunch of stamens whose filaments are thin and flexible so that they too shake in the wind. On fine, dry days, clouds of pollen are released and carried through the canopy perchance to land on a female flower of the same species. Most pollen will be lost by the wayside.

Female catkins are sometimes similar to the male, but in most species the female flowers are fewer in number and their most obvious feature is a tuft of feathery stigmas designed to sift pollen out of the wind. Although both male and female inflorescences usually occur on the same tree (monoecious), the females normally flower later than the males. (This may also happen within the bisexual flower of entomophilous, or insect-pollinated, species.) This staggering of sexual maturity is a step towards reducing, but not eliminating, the chances of self-pollination and the potential disadvantages of inbreeding. The next step in guaranteeing cross-pollination is the separation of the sexes on distinct male and female trees (dioecious), as with the willows and Holly.

FRUIT

The ultimate purpose of flowers is to produce seeds. Once the gametes have fused and the embryo is initiated, the tiny ovule develops into a seed that, when ripe and mature, is capable of germinating into a new plant. The ovary wall develops in ways that enhance the protection of the seeds and aid their dispersal. The ovary wall becomes the fruit wall.

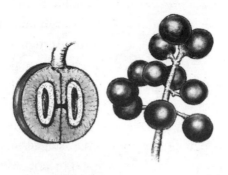

Berries

Some fruit walls become sweet and succulent, and attractive to birds and mammals. These are the **berries** – see the Wild Privet berries above. Generally, the seed wall is tough or indigestible, such that the seeds pass through the gut unharmed and get deposited some distance from the parent plant. Examples of trees that bear berries include the buckthorns and Wild Privet.

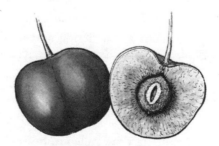

Drupes

The inner part of fleshy *Prunus* fruit walls, like those in cherries and Blackthorn, become woody and form tough, protective 'stones' around the seeds. Botanists call these **drupes**. Less obvious drupes include Elder, Guelder-rose, Dogwood and Holly, all of which contain very small stones.

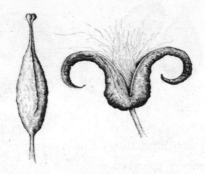

Capsules

The succulent fruits are those we immediately visualise when we think of fruits, but more commonly the ovary/fruit wall becomes dry. In **capsules**, these dry walls split open to release seeds. In willows and poplars, these are tiny and plumed, to drift far and wide on air currents.

Other dry fruits are single-seeded and don't split open. These include achenes, nuts and nutlets.

Achenes

When these are small, they are called **achenes**. Birch achenes develop wings that help carry them on the wind for long distances.

Nuts

When they are large, they contain plenty of protein or starch nourishment in the seed to feed the developing seedling – oak and hazel produce nourishing **nuts**. This nourishment is attractive to birds and mammals that collect the nuts and cart them off, frequently dropping or burying them and hence dispersing them.

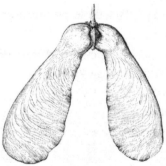

Winged Nutlets

Then there are several nuts that are sufficiently small to travel some distance by wind with the aid of a wing formed by either the ovary/fruit wall or by an associated bract: the **winged nutlets**. These include the maples and Ash (winged fruit walls), and Hornbeam and the limes (winged bracts – these are derived from modified leaves at the base of the flower stalk).

False Fruit

There is one other group of fruits – the **false fruits**. These are characteristic of the Rosaceae, notably Hawthorn, apple, Rowan and the other *Sorbus* species. Botanists call these fruits false because it is the hypanthium (tip of the flower stem), not the ovary wall, that swells into the attractive succulent part that surrounds the relatively undeveloped fruit walls of the dry true fruits within. See Rosaceae (page 178) for more details. Sea Buckthorn is another succulent false fruit which is comparable to the fruit of a Hawthorn, but contains a tiny achene inside, rather than a nutritious nut.

Every family is typified by a particular floral design and general strategy of pollination. There also tends to be a similarity in the type of fruit produced by each species in the family.

Where does the energy come from to achieve all this? What means do trees have to attract particular pollinators and dispersal agents? How do they defend themselves from browsing animals, pests, diseases and other hazards? Some of these questions can be answered by considering their chemistry.

3

The Chemistry
of Plants

THIS IS THE equation that summarises what is unarguably the most important chemical reaction on Earth:

$$6CO_2 + 6H_2O \rightarrow C_6H_{12}O_6 + 6O_2$$

carbon dioxide + water → glucose + oxygen

This reaction combines carbon dioxide and water to form energy-rich glucose, the simplest form of carbohydrate, upon which almost all life on Earth depends. Without carbohydrates, life as we know it would not be possible.

The reaction takes place in the green tissues of plants and is made possible only in the presence of the green pigment chlorophyll; it requires energy from the sun, which is then trapped within the carbohydrate molecule; the reaction is called photosynthesis.

It is the release of the energy trapped in the glucose molecule which provides the power required – not just by the plant, but by almost all life – to carry out all their daily functions: for plants to grow and reproduce; and for fungi and animals (including humans), who consume the glucose in plants. Even carnivores ultimately derive all their energy from plants via the herbivores lower in the food chain.

Carbon dioxide enters the plant – a tree, in our case – through the tiny pores, or stomata, on the surface of the leaves. Water is absorbed by the roots and is transported to the leaves by the xylem vessels of the stem and leaf veins.

Photosynthesis (creating glucose) takes place in the green tissues of the leaves. Glucose is then transported around the plant, in the phloem vessels of the veins of stems and roots, to where it is needed to provide energy for metabolic activity. It is used as building material for creating new tissues or stored as starch or oils for future energy needs.

Glucose provides building blocks, along with nitrogen and other elements obtained from the soil, to create all other major plant constituents, referred to as their 'primary metabolites': starches, proteins and lipids (oils). All three are found in all plants.

SPECIALISED METABOLITES

Plants also produce over 50,000 'specialised metabolites' (often referred to as 'secondary metabolites', a term that understates their remarkable properties and the unique roles they play). Although the specialised metabolites may not be fundamental to survival like the primary metabolites are, they serve a variety of functions to enhance the life of the plant, each one conferring an evolutionary advantage. Not all are produced by all plants – most plants focus on just a few. Some are toxins used by plants to deter predation by herbivorous animals or pathogenic fungi; others might manifest themselves as pigments or volatile and scented oils designed, for example, to attract insects for pollination. Many of them have properties that benefit humans if consumed as part of the wider diet. Even those that are toxic can have medicinal benefits if taken in controlled doses.

It is the specialised metabolites that often provide the memorable, useful and sometimes dangerous characteristics of different plant families and individual species.

The subject of specialised metabolites is populated with a huge number of seemingly unrelated terms that you may have heard, particularly if you are interested in topics surrounding medicine, healthy food and aromatherapy. If you enjoy the marvels of organic chemistry, you will be disappointed not to find more detail here. But there is really not the space to explore the complexities of the subject so I have decided to keep the language of chemistry to a minimum. For those who 'have always hated chemistry' please don't be put off by the occasional chemical term. You will generally find that the sentence makes sense if you ignore them.

To introduce the subject, I have highlighted four of the key terms – alkaloids, glycosides, terpenes and polyphenols – along with some relevant examples of each, most of which are associated with our trees and are referred to again in the species profiles later in the book. Note that the terms 'alkaloids', 'glycosides', 'terpenes' and 'polyphenols' are not all mutually exclusive from a chemistry perspective, which is why, for example, I refer to a terpene glycoside.

Alkaloids

There are over 21,000 alkaloids produced by plants, globally. Each alkaloid has a unique chemical structure. They usually taste bitter, are toxic to other organisms, and are used by the plant as grazing deterrents. Some famous *plant* alkaloids act on the central nervous system and thus have potential in traditional and modern medicine as analgesics, antihypertensives, tranquilisers, etc. Mankind has used alkaloids as stimulants (e.g. caffeine) or depressants (e.g. morphine) or for psychoactive experiences (e.g. cocaine) for thousands of years.

There is not a lot of evidence among our tree species of alkaloid occurrence. Globally, wind-pollinated families, including a third of our trees, tend not to produce alkaloids. But they do occur in conifers, notably the strong cardiotoxic, taxine alkaloids of Yew, *Taxus baccata*. They are located in the leaves and seeds and are therefore very effective anti-grazing chemicals. Globally, there seems to be a higher incidence of alkaloid occurrence in the more primitive families of plants that are listed early in the classification system. In this group we have only one member – Box, *Buxus sempervirens*. One of its active ingredients is cyclobuxine, a steroidal alkaloid that occurs in the leaves and bark. This alkaloid has recently been studied for the treatment of HIV/AIDS and may have potential for Alzheimer's and other conditions. Most alkaloids are lethally toxic in the wrong doses.

Polyphenols

There are over 7,000 polyphenols (aka phenolics). They include tannins and all the soluble so-called flavone pigments, some of which are antipathogenic, but most of which absorb damaging ultraviolet radiation and are used to attract and/or to deter. Of these, it is the anthocyanin pigments which give elderberries, and especially the dark cherries, their deep purple colour that attracts dispersal agents such as thrushes. Animals that enjoy consuming these fruits are seeking energy-rich sugars. They also benefit from associated nutrients including, in this case, the antioxidant qualities of the anthocyanins. Animals learn to associate the colour with the reward.

Tannins that give Crab Apples (particularly unripe apples) their bitterness are also phenolics. In this case the unpalatability prevents premature dispersal, before the seed is fully ready. The leaves, bark, wood and acorns of oak trees are famously rich in tannin, which acts as an effective inhibitor of fungal growth and hence decomposition. This has implications regarding carbon sequestration and the durability of timber. Oak timber is highly esteemed for its rot resistance.

Tannins have many diverse uses. Some of the polyphenol chemicals released from decomposing Sycamore leaves deter the germination and growth of young plants nearby. This competitive behaviour is known as allelopathy.

Glycosides

There are around 500 plant glycosides, which are a means for plants to store toxins in an inactive state until needed.

The toxin is attached to a sugar molecule, which renders it inactive. When the leaf or another structure is damaged or infected, plant enzymes cause the sugar part to be broken off, thus activating the toxin. Cyanogenic glycosides protect the seeds of the Rose family, notably Bird Cherry, by releasing hydrogen cyanide if damaged. Normally, the seed is rejected or passes through the gut unharmed – it is the fleshy surrounding fruit that is consumed. The iridoid glycoside of Dogwood (and many species in closely related families) deters grazers great and small, and the same chemical has been used pharmacologically as an effective anti-inflammatory. Despite the harmless, nutritious and fleshy outer seed coat (or aril) of Spindle, the seeds within are extremely toxic to birds and mammals, including man. They contain a cardiac glycoside (a terpene glycoside) and various other terpenes (see below). If consumed by humans, the concentration of these chemicals can cause severe liver and kidney damage and even death.

More famously, poplars and willows produce a glycoside called salicin, which is the natural precursor of the world's first synthetic drug – the analgesic we know as aspirin. If the willow is damaged or infected, salicin breaks down to release salicylic acid (a phenolic). This chemical is not itself a toxin, but a hormone that triggers the production of other toxic or unpalatable defence chemicals (mostly terpenes) to suppress the infection.

Simultaneously, volatile esters of salicylic acid are emitted by the infected plant. These diffuse through the atmosphere and are quickly detected by other plants of the same and different species, which are in turn triggered to produce defensive chemicals in advance of a likely pathogenic attack. It was first thought that the release of the volatile esters was an inevitable chemical side effect which, by chance, resulted in a totally unintended warning to the neighbouring plants. But scientists now believe that there is deliberate communication going on here. This is the subject of much research. Meanwhile, many other studies of organic substances emitted by plants have demonstrated they too can be detected by neighbouring plants and elicit appropriate responses.

Terpenes

Terpenes are a diverse class of over 15,000 organic compounds, and for these I will provide a snippet of chemistry.

Their basic component is an isoprene unit, a chemical that consists of five carbon atoms joined together. The simplest terpenes have just two isoprene units linked together and are known as monoterpenes. These have the chemical formula $C_{10}H_{16}$, are generally liquid in their pure form at room temperature and provide aromas, such as floral scents. The larger the number of isoprene units, the less volatile the terpene, so these don't contribute aroma. The tetraterpenoids, which are made up of eight isoprene units are too 'heavy' to be volatile. They include the pigments collectively known as carotenoids. As you can see, the number of isoprene units making up a terpene is indicated by a prefix – so mono-terpene (two isoprene units), di-terpene (four isoprene units).

Terpenes are the major components of resins that seal wounds and immobilise pathogens (and gum up insects' mouthparts). The associated odour warns potential pathogens. Resins are produced by most conifers, except Yew. But Yew does contain a different terpene, a diterpene called paclitaxel, which is used by the tree to deter or destroy pathogenic fungi and pharmaceutically to create a powerful chemotherapy drug. Terpenes are the primary constituents of the essential oils that give Juniper its characteristic aroma and protect it from bacterial attack. These oils have been used pharmaceutically for similar purposes. Volatile essential oils are what contribute to the various scents of flowers, and are used widely in traditional and alternative therapies, such as aromatherapy. The toxic iridoids present in Dogwood, *Viburnum*, Wild Privet and others are derived from monoterpenes. Sesquiterpenes (which contain three isoprene units) include farnesol, which contributes part of the scent of Lime (and other) flowers. It helps to enhance the volatility of the other floral aromas and is a pheromone to attract insect pollinators. And, as a side-line, it is also antibacterial.

High volumes of terpenes are released by trees in warm weather. They are thought to act as a natural means of cloud seeding, so stimulating rain. Clouds also help to keep the forest cool on hot days by intercepting strong sunlight.

The carotenoid pigments that contribute significantly to autumn colour are examples of tetraterpenoids. Unlike flavone pigments, they are not soluble in water. They play a supportive role in photosynthesis alongside chlorophyll, and they produce the red, yellow and orange colours of many of the Rosaceae fruit – notably Rowan, Whitebeam and Wild Service Tree. Carotenoids are present in leaves even in summer, although they are masked by the green pigment. Like flavone pigments, they are in leaves and fruit walls not simply to attract dispersal agents but also to provide protection from damaging ultraviolet radiation.

This brief review, that explores just some of the ways trees interact chemically with other organisms and the environment, illustrates another aspect of their huge diversity – a hidden world of complex lures and chemical warfare. But as we shall see in the next chapter, there is even more unseen and previously unsuspected activity going on that is vital to the life of trees.

4

The Importance
of Fungi

ONE OF THE excitements of a woodland walk in autumn is discovering Chanterelles, stinkhorns, earthstars, Penny Buns, Fly Agarics and a wealth of other toadstools on the forest floor. They are a reflection of some of the vital activity taking place out of sight in the soil and inside rotting wood. Toadstools are the fruiting bodies of fungi that exist below ground as mycelia – vast and incredibly valuable networks of microscopically fine hyphal threads. Without fungi, life on Earth, as we know it, would not be possible. Heard that before?

However, although fungi might be magic, like animals, they need a source of ready-made carbohydrates to fuel their energy demands. Many of the woodland fungi are saprophytes that scavenge for carbohydrates from dead bits of plants and animals. In so doing, they fill the essential role of helping to break down bulky organic material into humus (decomposed plant material), recycling nutrients back to the soil. Other organisms help, but saprophytic fungi play the major role.

Some fungi take this activity a step further and set-to on living trees (and other plants). These are the parasitic and pathogenic fungi. Most trees have evolved antifungal toxins to deter such infections, but weak specimens may succumb.

In the 1880s biologists became aware of another type of association between living plants and fungi – a symbiotic, or mutually beneficial, relationship. The fungus physically embraces and penetrates the finer roots of the tree with its mycelium and, via its huge network of hyphal threads, it effectively extends the capacity of the tree's root system to acquire water and a full range of nutrients from the soil. It can increase a tree's uptake of nutrients by over 80 per cent. In return the tree shares a large proportion, normally 20–30 per cent (sometimes up to 50 per cent or more) of its photosynthesised, energy-rich carbohydrates with the fungus. These symbiotic associations are called mycorrhizae, which means 'fungus roots'.

Globally, the vast majority of plants and innumerable species of fungi engage in these mycorrhizal relationships. The partnership has been operating since plants first migrated onto land about 460 million years ago (mya). Without the aid of fungi, it is highly unlikely that plants would ever have taken that first huge step. Today, three or four different types of mycorrhizae are recognised, each one filling a different niche. Arbuscular mycorrhizae (AM) are the basic and most commonly occurring type, involving 80 per cent of plants globally.

The type that concerns us most here is called ectomycorrhiza (EcM), which is thought to have evolved 156 mya.

It occurs mostly in the Arctic-Boreal and the Temperate zones of the world, where 100 per cent and 50 per cent of plant species, respectively, are involved. It is much more effective than AM in giving participating plants a huge survival advantage on nutrient-poor and comparatively cold and arid soils. (AM works better on deep, moist, nitrogen-rich soils.) In temperate regions EcM involves mostly trees and, unsurprisingly, these trees are the major players in all woodland communities. Twenty-five of our 52 species are EcM species. They include the pioneers and those that are most dominant and commonly occurring. They are listed below in their family groups.

Betulaceae: Silver and Downy Birch, Alder, Hornbeam and Hazel

Fagaceae: Sessile and Pedunculate Oak, Beech and Sweet Chestnut

Pinaceae: Scots Pine (and others, e.g. larches, firs, spruces)

Salicaceae: our two poplars and eight willows (plus many more)

Malvaceae: only the three limes (no other Malvaceae are EcM)

Rosaceae: only Rowan and then only sometimes

Some of these are also involved in AM associations, notably Alder and some of the Salicaceae.

Chanterelle
Associated with birch

Penny Bun
Associated with oak

Fly Agaric
Associated with birch & pine

Until recently, little more was known about mycorrhizae. Now the topic has become a major branch of scientific research. Work initiated in the Canadian forests during the 1990s revealed that EcM is a much more sophisticated and significant association than anyone ever imagined. Much of what follows applies to all types of mycorrhizal partnerships. EcM is most efficient in temperate regions: mycelia of EcM fungi extend furthest, in some cases to over 100 metres, and, like saprophytic fungi, many EcM fungal partners are capable of breaking down organic material to access more nutrients.

The fungi associated with different host trees link up so that all the mycorrhizal trees in the forest are connected via a vast network of fungal hyphae – the aptly termed 'Wood Wide Web'. This connectivity was first demonstrated using radioactive isotopes of carbon in the carbon dioxide that was 'fed' to young trees. The movement of carbon that was converted to photosynthesised sugars could be traced. Since then, some remarkable discoveries have been made:

- Sugars pass via the roots and mycorrhizae between trees of the same and different species so long as they are linked in to the EcM network.

- Mature trees appear to selectively support seedlings of their own kind before passing surplus sugars on to other species. (Or are the seedlings especially equipped to tap their own kind?)

- If one tree of any species is deprived of adequate light (and therefore unable to photosynthesise effectively), it is supported by sugars supplied by other trees of any species via the mycorrhizae. (Or is the fungus actually controlling an even distribution of fuel for itself?)

- If trees don't provide enough carbohydrate to the mycorrhizal fungi, the fungi can become parasitic or pathogenic; and if the trees get extra nutrients from artificial fertilisers, they reduce the carbohydrate given to the mycorrhizal fungi, and even try to get rid of them.

Birch has been shown to support conifer saplings struggling under the shade of a woodland canopy during summer months. In other seasons, the roles are reversed. This way, using the mycorrhizal network, differences between the strong and the weak are equalised. The whole community is supported and the whole ecosystem is kept in balance. With this in mind, one's view may change: what was once a beautiful solitary tree standing graceful, proud and unfettered, becomes a sad, lonely and vulnerable individual when one recognises that it is not part of an intimate and supportive mycorrhizal network.

All this seemingly altruistic behaviour of each mycorrhizal tree is actually to its species' long-term benefit. If it were to competitively exclude all other species to achieve a monoculture, disease could spread rapidly through the forest and wipe it out completely. In a mixed forest, if there is a localised outbreak of disease that affects 'species A', the unaffected surrounding tree species may isolate individuals of 'species A' from infection and will continue to maintain the forest environment so that the seeds of the affected individuals of 'A' will be able to re-establish.

Other benefits that the fungal partners confer on the host trees include protecting the tree from toxicity in the soil. Fungi are more tolerant of toxins than trees are. They are able to decompose some and sequester others, store them and excrete them by concentrating them in their ephemeral toadstools. Mycorrhizal fungi also provide physical and chemical defences against root pathogens and predators, as well as chemically stimulating the tree to manufacture its own particular defence from a repertoire of tannins, phenols, carotenoids, etc.

Yet another remarkable phenomenon that operates via mycorrhizae is the transmission of messages from tree to tree. These typically take the form of chemical signals to warn of a pathogen attack. Some are released as volatile esters from the leaves and are dispersed randomly according to the direction of the wind, but others are transmitted via the Wood Wide Web so that all trees that are linked are prepared, and respond by manufacturing defence chemicals in advance of the likely attack.

Trees also produce electrical signalling in response to environmental challenges such as wounding, a rise in salinity or drought. These signals travel via the same underground internet as pulses at 1 cm per second. This is painfully slow by human standards, but not for naturally long-lived trees.

Different species of fungi in the partnerships are responsible for fulfilling different roles in the mycorrhizal system. Some also produce energy-rich exudates that feed bacteria, enabling them to perform their roles in the soil. Gel-like mycorrhizal exudates increase the volume of water that the soil can hold, simultaneously halving the loss of nutrients through leaching. In so many ways, the fungi improve soil conditions for all plants, not just those involved in the partnerships.

The fungal partner receives energy-rich carbohydrates in return for all its services. It also ensures a stable forest environment, with a diversity of tree species to serve as alternative hosts if one species dies out. It is quite probable that fungi are the controlling beneficiaries of diversity in a mature forest. And it is highly likely that the widespread deterioration of the health of trees across Europe in recent decades has been exacerbated by steady destruction of their mycorrhizal networks. This could be due to inappropriate land management that has not taken mycorrhizae into account, such as ploughing and the use of fertilisers, herbicides, fungicides, etc. Hopefully, we are learning to do better.

Tree-spotting

Researchers can explain the complex interactions of mycorrhizae in scientific terms. But one doesn't need to understand the science in order to recognise that the end result is that the major players in the woodland community are communicating with each other and responding in supportive and cooperative ways. *Homo sapiens* could learn a lot from the way natural forests work. Most scientists argue that this cooperation between trees only works when it is in their own self-interests (or the interests of those sharing their genes – the 'selfish gene'). Others envisage a kind of trading of mutual respect between species. Either way, words like 'connected', 'reciprocity', 'balance', 'kinship', 'complexity' and 'adaptability' apply to the forest community, but cannot often be applied when humans get involved. This species has too strong a sense of its own supreme entitlement.

So, when conservationists argue so fiercely that 'ancient woodland' should be protected, it is not just the trees and the above ground wealth of biodiversity that they are trying to retain but this complex, hidden community of plants and fungi and other organisms beneath the soil.

5

The History of
Britain's Forests

NOW THAT WE have considered some of the interactions that determine how trees survive and thrive in
our temperate environment, it is easier to understand how
the natural forests of the British Isles have developed and
changed since the last Ice Age. In this chapter we explore how
trees responded to the opportunity for colonisation and how
they coped with the environmental forces at play. And we also
learn how botanists interpret 'native' in this context.

Ice sheets and glaciers started to spread across most of
Britain about 2.6 mya, eliminating 'all' life as they did so.
Certainly the forest communities were obliterated across most
of the landscape. The palette was wiped clean. Eventually,
around 11,600 years ago, the last of the ice sheets began to
retreat, and the British islands could be populated by trees
once again.

THE TERTIARY PERIOD

But first, let's consider a time long before this – 65 million years ago. The land that we now call the British Isles was covered in tropical rainforest, dominated by flowering trees that can still be found in the forests of the tropics of Southeast Asia today. We know this from datable fossils that have been found in the London Clay that was laid down at this time. This was the start of what geologists call the Tertiary period of the Cenozoic era.

Towards the end of the Tertiary, the climate of Western Europe (and indeed the whole world) had become increasingly colder – terminating in the onset of the Pleistocene Ice Age, 2.6 million years ago). Most of the tropical species had gradually migrated to warmer climes towards the equator. But in Europe, unlike in eastern Asia and the Americas, the east–west alignment of the ice-capped mountain ranges hindered their escape southwards. Those tropical species that were already south of the mountain chains found refuge and managed to flourish in a semi-tropical climate that prevailed in a few suitable, sheltered, south-facing valleys around the Mediterranean Sea and on the Atlantic islands of the Azores, the Canaries and Madeira, where tiny remnants of semi-tropical forest are still found today. This type of forest is called laurisilva, and is typified by trees with evergreen leathery leaves, including Bay, *Laurus nobilis*, which gives the forest its name.

THE PLEISTOCENE EPOCH

During the Ice Age, the climate of Europe became not only bitterly cold but very dry. Deep layers of ice capped the highlands and much of the lowlands in the north as well. Sea levels dropped as water was held in vast ice sheets and glaciers. The continental shelves were exposed, including the bed of what is now the North Sea, such that the British Isles became part of mainland Europe. The prevailing winds in Western Europe swept in from the frozen lands of northern Asia in the east.

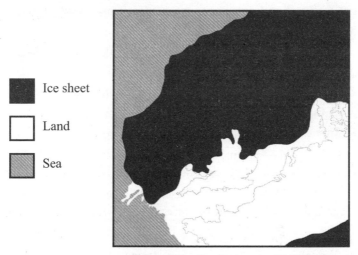

Start of the Ice Retreat c.11,600 BP

The lowlands that were not covered in deep ice sheets and glaciers (including most of what is now the North Sea and the south of mainland Britain) supported a remarkable and sparse community of plants that had escaped the ice caps of the mountains to both the south and to the north. This bleak tundra landscape was dominated not by trees but by low-growing sedges and grasses and a variety of prostrate shrubs, few of which will ever grow as a tree even if cultivated in warmer climes.

Over the course of two and a half million years, there were four main glacial phases, separated by three interglacial periods when the ice melted and the climate warmed up again – not to tropical temperatures, but generally warmer than today. During each interglacial, trees and other plants slowly migrated back to Britain mainly from the south, crossing the broad valley between the Continent and south-east England and also across the exposed bed of what is now the North Sea via Doggerland.

Each time the next glacial phase approached, the forests were slowly obliterated, and the tree species retreated to warmer lowlands further south. Arctic-alpine species moved down to the exposed lowlands of Britain again, until they too became overwhelmed by deep layers of ice.

During the interglacial periods of the Ice Age, Palaeolithic hunter-gatherers were among the mammals that returned to Britain, but not apparently during the final interglacial. Instead, they hung out in the lowlands of continental Europe.

POST GLACIAL – THE HOLOCENE PERIOD

The last retreat of the ice started 11,600 years before present (BP), and many geologists would suggest that we are currently part way through yet another interglacial called the 'Flandrian', and would be heading for another glacial phase, were it not for human-induced global warming. Let's now consider the changes in vegetation that have occurred over the last 11,600 years since the glaciers' final retreat.

THE PIONEERS

Once the glaciers started to pull back, they revealed a wide, open landscape ripe for colonisation. But initially, this landscape was not enticing for plants.

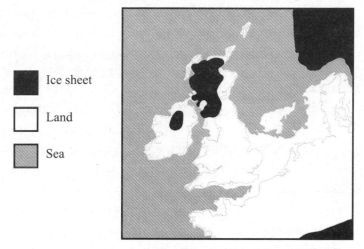

Ice sheet

Land

Sea

Ice Retreat & Rising Sea c.9000 BP

Bitterly cold and dry Arctic winds swept across this permanently frozen desert landscape of bare rock and frozen rock debris which offered little available water or nutrients. The ground was totally devoid of moisture-retaining, nutrient-rich humus, and water was inaccessible in its frozen state. So how could plants establish a foothold in this landscape?

- To take full advantage of this vast – yet unappealing – opportunity, the pioneer species would need to get in fast – wind dispersal.

- If this new terrain was less than ideal for plants, it was even more inhospitable for animals, including pollinating insects. So in order to be successful, the early pioneers would need to be pollinated by the wind, of which there was plenty.

- To succeed in this harsh barren environment, the pioneers would need to keep a low profile out of the wind and enlist the help of fungi – and especially those that happily join in ectomycorrhizal associations.

The candidates that were perfectly suited included the sedges, grasses and the many dwarf shrubs of the tundra community. Notable among these would have been the dwarf willows, birch, juniper, and many ericaceous shrubs. Following in their wake, the pioneer tree species included Aspen, taller willows and predominantly Downy Birch, followed by Scots Pine – trees of cold, dry climates. Both the tundra species and the pioneer trees were wind-dispersed, predominantly wind-pollinated and associated with ectomycorrhizal fungi. There was in fact one tree among the initial treeless tundra community: Sea Buckthorn. It can stand 6 metres tall, but in extreme conditions it adopts a prostrate habit. It does not associate with ectomycorrhizal fungi, but it does engage in an arbuscular mycorrhizal partnership and also a symbiotic association with a species of nitrogen-fixing bacteria of the genus *Frankia*. What a significant role Sea Buckthorn must have played in these impoverished soils by increasing the nutrient availability for the trees that followed.

By 9000 BP, Mesolithic hunter-gatherers had made their way to Britain and roamed this early, sparsely wooded Flandrian landscape, hunting animals and collecting roots, berries and seeds.

THE FOREST RETURNS

During the Flandrian, as the climate in Britain became warmer, water was released from the frozen soil. Alder and willows spread from the south and east and settled into the wet hollows and valley bottoms. Hazel found plenty of sunny clearings in the birch and pine forests and gradually expanded its range around 10,500 BP. Soon more and more different species of trees filtered in, in low numbers, supported by the birch and their shared ectomycorrhizal associates. Oak and Wych Elm were among the first to appear and spread northwards along with the others. Initially, the tundra species lived in harmony with the sparse, open birch forest, but as more trees joined the scene, the denser shade drove the tundra community of Arctic-alpines further north and up to higher ground where it still exists today, at the tops of the Scottish mountains. Alternatively, many tundra species were driven out to the exposed, salt-sprayed coasts. Sea Buckthorn took the latter route.

Trees migrated northwards, particularly up the western side of the country, where the proximity of the Atlantic created the warmest conditions. On the heels of the pioneers, some of the Scots Pine travelled along this route, reaching northwest Scotland by 8500 BP, pushing the tundra community before it. Another migration route led from the east, bringing Scots Pine to Britain via Doggerland.

Meanwhile, other plant species continued to spread into southern and eastern Britain but, with the forest cover closing in, newcomers found it harder to find a space. It was OK for shade-tolerant woodland species, but there was not much scope for plants of open, sunny habitats. By 7000 BP the climate in the south of Britain had become decidedly warmer and wetter. Around this time the diverse, deciduous, broad-leaved mixed oak forests, for which Britain is so famous, became established and started to spread northwards.

THE ATLANTIC PERIOD 7000–5000 BP

The Atlantic period, from 7000–5000 BP, was one of warm, wet summers and mild, wet winters. Most of the Scandinavian ice sheet had melted, sea levels had risen, and the North Sea had been gradually expanding southwards until it eventually broke through, into the Channel, decisively closing the land bridge between Europe and Britain. This put a stop to any further natural immigration of plant species. Even the narrow Straits of Dover are too wide to permit the dispersal of windborne seeds and fruits, and birds will empty their guts and undergo a thorough preening to remove hitch-hiking seeds and fruits before attempting such a long flight. From this time on, no more plant species entered the British Isles via means of natural dispersal (with the occasional exception of orchids, which have particularly tiny seeds).

The Atlantic climate that prevailed in Britain for over 2,000 years was warmer and wetter than it is today. These conditions, and the accumulating soils, were perfect for the deciduous broad-leaved trees that are so much part of the natural landscapes of much of the Britain Isles today. The mixed oak forests of the Atlantic period were most luxuriant in the south and also particularly in the west, far up into Scotland. In addition to oak and Wych Elm, many of our large trees – like Ash, Hornbeam, lime and Beech – played a significant role jostling for co-leadership (or sometimes leadership) in these flourishing mixed oak forests. While oak stretched as far as the Morar peninsula and even across to southwest Skye, lime did not manage it past the Lake District. Scots Pine established its stronghold in the Grampian Mountains and in much of northwest Scotland, though the extreme northwest remained largely treeless.

To the south of Britain, other regional differences developed. For example, Small-leaved Lime featured as a co-dominant in the southeast and East Anglia, while Ash, an archetypal Atlantic species, performed better in the west, particularly on limestone soils.

A number of trees never made it to Ireland. The Irish Sea, which separates Ireland from mainland Britain, flooded before the British mainland was separated from Europe. Particularly notable among the Irish absentees were Lime, Beech, Hornbeam and Field Maple. These 'continental' species were slow to enter southeast Britain, only penetrating north and west once the conditions were more favourable. By the time they had spread across Britain, they were too late to cross to Ireland. Conversely, Strawberry Tree, a Mediterranean species with close affinities to the semi-tropical laurisilva forests of the late Tertiary, was remarkable in returning via the Atlantic seaboard and crossing to southwest Ireland. Exactly when this happened, and via what precise route, has not yet been established. By contrast, Holly and Ivy, also with evergreen, leathery leaves and similar Mediterranean and laurisilva origins, managed to spread widely throughout the British Isles.

How do we know all this?

PALYNOLOGY

Details of the history of the changing vegetation of Britain during and since the Ice Age has been worked out by palaeobotanists. Since the early nineteenth century, palaeobotanists have been studying the fossil remains of plants embedded in datable geological deposits going back over 400 million years. Their work has supported studies regarding plant evolution, which in turn plays an important role in directing decisions that determine classification systems that are based on evolutionary relationships – including the one used today and in this book.

Towards the end of the nineteenth century, one branch of palaeobotany embraced palynology, or the study of dust-sized particles, which in this case meant pollen grains. The outer coats of pollen grains are immensely durable and the grains of each species are patterned uniquely, making them commonly identifiable at species level.

Hay-fever sufferers will be acutely aware that at certain times of the year, the air is full of wind-dispersed pollen grains, invisible to most of us but detectable by those who suffer an allergic reaction to the particular protein associated with specific pollen species. The pollen grains that do not end up on compatible stigmas or inside sensitive noses, i.e. most of them, fall to the ground or on to the surface of ponds and lakes, where they eventually sink and become incorporated into the peat. They do so along with other plant remains, including a shower of pollen from all the other species in the landscape surrounding the lake at the time. Some peat deposits have built up over many thousands of years,

Oak

Scots Pine

Wild Cherry

Alder

Field Maple

Holly

Sizes: 0.028–0.078mm

incorporating a record of the changes in the surrounding vegetation.[4] Carbon dating techniques provide a means of putting a date to each step in those changes. What a fantastic resource to enable us to reconstruct past environments and ecosystems.

A fascinating line of research, but laborious work. The palynologist first drills out a core of peat or lake sediment from a deposit, generally 5–10 metres deep (but often much deeper); they then take minute samples from different depths, keeping some from each sample for carbon dating. Extracting the pollen from the sediment sample generally takes a day of careful treatments, including boiling the sample in concentrated hydrofluoric acid, which indicates that the coat of these pollen grains is extremely resilient – this acid dissolves even quartz grains.

The extracted pollen samples are placed on microscope slides. Then palynologists spend months – no, years – patiently exploring slide after

---

4 Wind-pollinated plants will inevitably be better represented than those whose pollen is transported by insects. Such disparities are accounted for during the data analysis.

slide with binocular microscopes. Painstakingly long hours searching through microscopic plant debris, looking for pollen grains (a daily total of possibly 500 grains), identifying them and keeping a tally of each species found in each layer. They do this day after day after day. I know, because one of my best friends at university went on to research for a PhD thesis on the vegetation history of the Isle of Skye. The work that Will and others did confirmed the western passage of the pioneer trees, which paved the way for oak to penetrate northwards up the Atlantic seaboard, before establishing itself in Scotland.[5]

Electron microscopes (which take exquisite pictures you can find on the internet) were not used by Will, and were certainly not around in the early 1900s when most of this early research was going on. The intricate detail needed for accurate identification was hard to determine and required immense patience.

FOREST DECLINE
5000 BP TO PRESENT DAY

During the warm wet Atlantic period, Mesolithic people had to change their lifestyle from one of wide-roaming hunters of the open plains of the tundra landscape to either becoming forest dwellers or retreating to the edges of the forest – along the riverbanks or the coast where they could rely more easily on fish and birds for their protein supply. This gave rise to a more settled lifestyle.

5   Birks, H.J.B and Williams,W. 1983. Late-Quaternary vegetational history of the Inner Hebrides. Proceedings of the Royal Society of Edinburgh, 83B. 269–292.

The History of Britain's Forests

Around 5000 BP there was an abrupt change in the pollen record – a dramatic decline of elm followed by another more gradual and temporary decline of the other major forest constituents – oak, lime, Ash, etc. Simultaneously, there was a marked but temporary increase in the pollen of grasses and weed species, followed by a peak in the pollen of a large number of shrub species, before a gradual return to natural high forest species again. This pattern is reflected at similar-aged sites throughout northwest Europe. Associated with this abrupt and consistent change is evidence of fire in the form of charcoal layers and ash deposits in the peat. Fire is unusual in wet Atlantic climates. So the widespread occurrence of wood ash had to be attributable to human activity – and artefacts of Neolithic cultures were discovered from contemporary arch-aeological sites nearby.

Neolithic farmers from southeast Europe had made their way to the British coast, where they integrated comfortably into the local lifestyle and brought with them the techniques and equipment for clearing patches of woodland using fire. They then cultivated cereals on the land, which had been enriched with potash from the burnt vegetation.

The fact that the forest clearance at any one site was only temporary in the pollen record is in accord with the practice of primitive arable farming. Once the fertility of the soil was exhausted, the site was abandoned and another patch of forest was cleared. Full regeneration of high forest trees would take place within 200 years, which tallies neatly with the pollen and carbon-dating evidence. But this time Ash got a head start on the oak in many places, particularly in the west. It had retained its dominance at suitable sites until the fungal disease *Hymenoscyphus fraxineus*, commonly known as Chalara, that caused ash dieback early in the twenty-first century.

Forest clearance continued at this violent but partially recoverable pace for the next 2,000 years, into the Bronze Age. In some areas where the soils were light and easy to cultivate, the forest never did recover and today certain extensive areas of open grassland and heathland in the south of England are considered to have originated from these early farming activities. The Breckland of East Anglia and the chalk downs of southeast England are examples. Species-rich scrubland also appeared at this time and persisted, particularly in areas which had been cleared for grazing domestic stock and that continued to be grazed, if only intermittently, thenceforward. Species such as Field Maple, Spindle, Buckthorn and Whitebeam appeared more significantly in the pollen record at this time, while Hawthorn, Elder and Blackthorn (though present before) greatly extended their range.

The abrupt elm decline that preceded the more general forest decline described above has long been a puzzle to palynologists. Interestingly, the former occurred at almost exactly the same time at sites all over Britain, while the latter followed the movements of the Neolithic farmers over a longer period. Recently, the elm decline has been put down to something akin to the devastating Dutch elm disease of the early 1970s.

Around 3000 BP (and earlier in the north), the general decline in forest cover took on a steeper curve. One reason for this downturn was a deterioration of the climate – cooler and wetter. This, in conjunction with forest clearance, had the combined impact of the development of extensive areas of blanket bog.[6] This was especially true in the uplands of Britain and much of the centre of Ireland. Blanket bog prevented the return of the natural woodland above about 300 metres (1,000 feet), which included much of what had been the Caledonian pine forest region of Scotland.

This period also coincides with the advent of the Iron Age and the use of stronger tools made of iron. For this, people needed charcoal in abundance for smelting that iron to turn into tools – to cut down more trees and enable the ploughing of heavier soils. On the heavy Wealden clays of Kent, Hornbeam was actually cultivated in favour of other species because it makes especially good charcoal, and the Hornbeam-dominated woods remain to this day. The arable farmers were keen to turn to the richer, heavier soils; they abandoned the acid uplands of the north and west, which resulted in the expansion of treeless moorland, as on Dartmoor. They also abandoned the thin soils of the chalk and limestone of the uplands of southern Britain. This gave Beech its first opportunity to dominate. Today, our most famous Beech woods still cling to the hilltop plateaux of places like Burnham Beeches in the Chilterns and in patches along the crest of the chalk downs.

Forest destruction continued apace over subsequent centuries. Even when adequate forest had been cleared for farming, there were other major demands on the forest trees – timber for building, shipbuilding, furniture, tool heads and

---

6   The climate-induced retreat of forest and development of blanket bogs was exacerbated where Neolithic farmers cleared trees for farming. Where the cleared land fell into disuse, the soil began to leach its nutrients and become more acidic. Wet, acidic soils are suitable for the growth of ericaceous shrubs, sedges, rushes and bog mosses (*Sphagnum*). The organic debris from these plants accumulated, undecomposed in the wet conditions, and deep layers of peat developed – blanket bog.

handles, and musical instruments, to name some of the most obvious. It is likely that the biggest and best trees of each species were always selected for harvesting, so the quality of the gene pool of current forest trees has almost certainly diminished over the centuries.

At one time, forest of one type or another covered nearly all of the British Isles (though there is evidence to suggest that plenty of open wood pasture also existed – maintained by herds of large wild herbivores). Due to human exploitation only 13 per cent of the land[7] is now covered in forest, and much of that is monoculture plantation forest. Only 2 per cent is 'semi-natural' forest. The timeline opposite summarises all the forest changes since the Ice Age.

One of the worrying aspects of climate change is the shrinking of the polar ice caps. A different perspective, one not often referred to, is the consequent migration of pioneer tree species northward to colonise previously unavailable territory. Unsurprisingly, it is the same pioneer species that led the way 11,600 years ago that are leading the advance today.

NATIVE VERSUS ALIEN SPECIES

The concept of a 'native' species is a useful one because it gives us a benchmark when considering the flora of our islands. 'Native' trees are considered to be those that migrated to Britain before the land bridge between us and Europe was flooded by the melting ice and we became an archipelago of

7   Office for National Statistics. (February 2020). *Woodland natural capital accounts.*
Department of Agriculture, Food and the Marine. (2020). *Forest Statistics Ireland 2020.*

Years BP	Climate/ technology	Activities/events, vegetation type	Significant tree species
0	Today	2% semi-natural forest remains	
300	Industrial Age **Sub-Atlantic period** cool/wet	Clearance continues 50% forest left	Many introduced species
2000 2700	Iron Age	Blanket bogs develop in north and west	
3000		Clearance continues	
	Bronze Age **Sub-Boreal period** cool/dry	Forest clearance from south to north	Increase in Ash and Beech Increase in shrubs: Elder, Hawthorn, Blackthorn, etc.
4500 5000	Neolithic	Widespread elm decline	Pine reaches max in Scotland ~4,000 then declines
	Atlantic period warm/wet	Channel forms Age of the limes Mixed oak forest (south) Birch-Pine (north)	Oak dominant with Wych Elm, Ash, Alder as far as northwest Scotland Lime significant with Hornbeam, Beech as far as Lake District
7000			Pine spreads into Scotland
	Mesolithic **Boreal period** cold/dry	Forest cover thickens	Oak and Wych Elm becoming dominant Hazel and Rowan
9000 0500	permafrost starts thawing in south	Open woodland, scattered trees	Willows and Alders (wet); Birch, Pine, Juniper (dry)
1600	**Ice Age ends** very cold/dry	Pioneer trees in south	Aspen, Downy Birch
4000	**Younger Dryas** very cold/dry	Ice cover in north Tundra in extreme south	Sea Buckthorn (no trees)

islands, around 7000 BP. But simply because a plant failed to get back into Britain after the last glacial phase does not necessarily mean that it has no right to be here. Many subsequent arrivals have slotted peacefully into our natural ecosystems. Botanists use the term 'alien' for those plants that did not manage to get in under their own steam, but were introduced deliberately or accidentally by man and may subsequently become established in the wild – naturalised.

Unfortunately, the notorious aggressive behaviour of some alien plant species has given all alien plants a bad name. Many of them are not aggressive – and anyway, many of our native species, such as Creeping Thistle, will behave 'aggressively' if given the appropriate conditions, (often disturbed, man-made). They are merely demonstrating their opportunistic potential. Conifers grown as timber crops, such as Sitka Spruce and Douglas Fir, are introduced species that occasionally escape into the wild like some garden plants. All are alien in that they did not reach the British Isles naturally.

Some of our native trees are on the brink of extinction, while others have been artificially increased by deliberate planting. In this book we include two species that were introduced comparatively recently, one of which has become more widespread and common than any of our native species. The irony now is that, with climate change, we may need to think again about species introductions from Europe. Some species may fill an important role in the sustainability of our plant communities, which is critical for the natural environment, our well-being and our economy.

6

Why Trees and Forests Are Important

ECOSYSTEM SERVICES

MANY OF US find it somewhat offensive to view trees as providing services. Surely it's more important simply to appreciate them for their beauty and to recognise their right to exist alongside us in this world. Nevertheless, it is sobering to consider how vital trees are – and have been for millions of years – in determining the health of the planet. Forests have been treated with such contempt by mankind, and we are only now beginning to understand the appalling damage we have caused, not least of all to global biodiversity. In Britain, a single oak tree provides food and shelter for hundreds of different creatures – invertebrates, birds, mammals – as well as a wealth of mosses, lichens and fungi. It's little wonder that ancient, undisturbed, natural woodlands are some of the most diverse habitats for wildlife in the world. The same cannot be said about monoculture plantations of non-native tree species, which are so frequently seen in our landscape.

In the species profile section of this book, we touch on the various products that can be obtained from different tree species – products such as nuts, berries, timber, fibres, fuel and dyes. We are no longer so intimately aware of, nor so directly dependent on, forest products as our ancestors were. However, scientists are still rediscovering 'new' and remarkable arboreal chemicals that feed pharmaceutical research. '**RE**discovering', because our ancestors discovered many of their medicinal properties by trial and error thousands of years ago.

The British Isles support a variety of native forests: not just the widely scattered, bluebell-carpeted, mixed oak forests, but also others that are dramatically different. For example, the Caledonian pine forests of the Scottish Highlands, the Alder swamps of the lowland floodplains, the Beech hangers of the chalk uplands, the moss-covered, twisted and gnarled Sessile Oaks of the dripping rainforests along our Atlantic seaboard. The tragedy is that what remains now are pitiful representations of their former selves, fragmented by deserts of arable land and urban sprawl. But we still need them and rely on them more than we realise. We, and the rest of life on Earth, depend on them as much as we depend on the tropical jungles that are being destroyed to make way for beef cattle, feed for livestock and oil palm plantations – or the mangrove swamps that are being cleared and drained for holiday resorts. It is important to recognise some of the fundamental ecological roles that are fulfilled so brilliantly by native trees and forests.

WHY TREES AND FORESTS ARE IMPORTANT

We are coming to understand the many organisms and habitats that combine to ensure that our atmosphere is not choking with carbon dioxide and depleted in oxygen. Plants, and trees in particular, are prominent among them. Trees absorb carbon dioxide during photosynthesis and release oxygen as a by-product. Forests are among the world's most important biomes that sequester carbon, a task that reduces global warming and climate change. We have discussed some of our current understanding of the amazing mycorrhizal systems. There is undoubtedly more to discover here but, in terms of sequestering carbon, it has been calculated that ecosystems with thriving mycorrhizal networks store eight times as much carbon as ecosystems without such networks. Every year billions of tons of carbon, in the form of dissolved sugars, flow from the trees to their fungal partners below ground.

One of the alarming consequences of climate change has been the devastating destruction caused by floods. These are particularly severe in places where forests have been cleared in the uplands; as a result, soil, with no vegetation to hold it in place, has been washed away – so removing the natural sponges of the landscape. The soil is washed downhill into the rivers, thus exacerbating the damage caused by floodwater in the lowlands. (On the high plateaux of north and northwest Britain, peat bogs replace forest cover. These act as excellent carbon sinks and highly efficient sponges, regulating the gradual release of water to the lowlands. But our upland peat bogs are also under threat.) The yearly United Nations Climate Change Conference (known as COP, for 'Conference of the Parties') summits are focusing more and more on all these matters.

Tree-spotting

Not only do forests regulate the gases in the atmosphere, but many trees also filter out airborne pollutants. It has been repeatedly demonstrated that 'green cities' are much healthier than those devoid of street trees and green parks. This brings us to another aspect of the importance of trees and woodland – the cultural perspective.

Our ancestors lived for thousands of years in a forested landscape. Although they tended to cling to the more open coastal and riverbank sites, their lives were dominated in many ways by the neighbouring forest – a source of good things, but potentially dangerous; a powerful place. A sense of respect was firmly embedded in our ancestral psyche – a respect that is still felt but interpreted in various ways by people today. The wildwood has played a significant role throughout human history. Most people value our remaining ancient woodlands, and their sense of permanence, as a sacrosanct yet dwindling part of our heritage. Many enjoy the opportunity to roam through, or play in, woodland landscapes – returning home at the end of the day with a sense of heightened health and well-being. This can be attributed simply to experiencing a day of energetic exercise and inhaling the clean atmosphere among the trees. But there's more – trees emit a cocktail of forest chemicals which, when inhaled, have been shown to revitalise our immune system.[8] Three days in the forest will give you 30 days of improved immunity.

There are also those who sense a different kind of enrichment from something less tangible, something stronger

8 Li Q (2010). Effect of forest bathing trips on human immune function. *Environmental health and preventive medicine*, 15(1), 9–17. doi.org/10.1007/s12199-008-0068-3

– or even, perhaps, as our ancestors thought, something spiritual.

There are many other topics that we could have explored, such as the vast range of highly specialised uses of forest products and the role that trees have played in our economic and political history. These are extraordinary and fascinating stories, as are the many myths and legends, in which trees play the lead roles. All those stories, and those we have told here, become much more compelling once we know the characters involved.

Walks in the countryside also take on a new dimension when you find yourself on familiar, first-name terms with the trees around you. Naming trees can be great fun and an end in itself. But it is more than that. Once you have the name, you have the key that opens the door to a wealth of information and a wider understanding.

PART TWO

IDENTIFICATION

7

Identifying Trees in Summer: Using Leaves

RECOGNITION VERSUS IDENTIFICATION

IN THE INTRODUCTION we considered some of the ways we recognise the trees we know. Each species (or genus) of tree has some characteristic feature that is distinctive. Often those distinctive features are the type of fruit, such as the acorns of oaks or the helicopters (or double samaras) of maples. Sometimes the fruit is so characteristic that it is synonymous with the name of the tree, notably in the Rosaceae – Bird **Cherry,** Crab **Apple, Haw**thorn.

People who are familiar with trees can recognise many species from a distance – something about the stance of each is characteristic. That 'something' is often intangible and sometimes referred to as the 'jizz'. If challenged, they might be pushed to justify what criteria they had used. But even experts often need to verify their hunch by getting closer to check out some distinctive features. In the absence of fruits, botanists will look for other key identification features – those that provide the 'key' to the plant's identity.

So what features can we use? Can we use the fruit? Despite their symbolic/iconic value, fruit cannot be relied upon. The fruits of most trees are attached to the tree for only a short time, and then that clue is lost. Flowers are even more transitory. And of course both flowers and fruits are often high on the tree and hard to see. So although floral and fruiting features are fundamental in classifying plants, they are not very helpful for identifying trees in the field.

Can we use the bark? As children, some of us were encouraged to make bark rubbings as a way to familiarise ourselves with the diversity of textures and patterns. There are several bark features that provide useful clues to identity, such as the white of birch bark, the horizontal splits of cherry bark and the diamond-shaped cracks on the trunks of some poplars. But in most cases, features of the bark are evident only in mature specimens, which doesn't help when one finds a young sapling. Even a fully grown but as yet still immature Ash tree retains its smooth juvenile bark. Only in its mature years does its bark become cracked and wrinkled, so the bark is not helpful.

However, the leaves do provide reliable features. Leaves are on the tree for more or less half the year and, despite being renewed each year, they retain their characteristic shape throughout the life of the tree.[9] So, we will start with a

---

9 Leaves of suckers and regrowth from the stump after felling tend to be exceptionally large, and sometimes take on a different shape. So avoid using these for ID, where possible.

straightforward way to identify trees based on the key features of their leaves, and in the next chapter, we will explore ways to identify them in the absence of leaves – during the winter months.

MAIN IDENTIFICATION FEATURES OF LEAVES

Leaves are a distinctive feature of most plants, and the leaves of each species are distinct from all others in many ways. Unsurprisingly, species that are closely related tend to have similar leaves, though not exactly alike. Spend a moment looking at these two obviously distinct specimens overleaf, and consider the various ways that they differ.

A Note on Hand Lenses

Some of the fine detail is easier to see if you use a hand lens. The best magnification for most botanical fieldwork is 10x. Do not be tempted by anything stronger. Unlike a magnifying glass (usually a strength of 3–5x), the diameter of the hand lens is small, and you need to hold it very close to your eye to get a wide field of view. Keep the lens close to your eye and bring the leaf as close as necessary until the parts you want to see (such as the hairs on the undersurface) are in perfect focus. This may seem tedious and like too much effort – but, actually, the detail that is revealed is compelling and opens the door to another world.

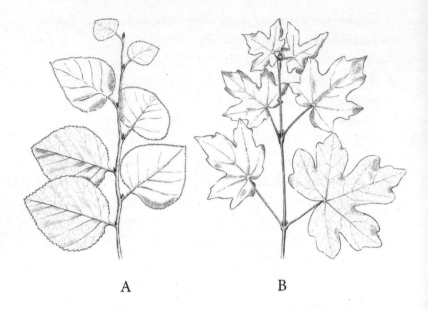

A   B

Notice the tiny buds that occur on the stem above the attachment of each leaf stalk and at the tip of the stem.

We'll call them species A and species B. There are two obvious ways in which the leaves differ – their basic shape and how they are attached to the stem.

1. The leaf shape of species A is simple in outline, whereas the leaves of B are deeply lobed. This type of lobing is referred to as palmate – meaning it usually has five lobes (but sometimes just three, or more than five) and the main veins of the leaf are palmately arranged, like the fingers attached to your palm. When the lobes occur like those of an oak leaf, the lobing is referred to

as pinnate, as are its main veins. (There are two other basic shapes – see the next page.)

2. The leaves of A are arranged alternately (or more strictly, they are attached spirally along the stem), whereas those of B are in opposite pairs, and each pair is attached at right angles to those above and below. (These are the only arrangements, though leaves arranged in a whorl of three can also occur. This is considered to be a modification of opposite pairs and is found in only one of our trees.)

There are other differences as well, such as:

- The leaves of A have short stalks (petioles), the leaf stalks of B are much longer.

- The margin of the leaf of A is serrated, whereas that of the lobed margin of B is unbroken, or 'entire'.

- The leaf, its stalk and the twig of A are sparsely hairy, while those of B are hairless (best detected with a hand lens).

- The colour of the leaves will also be different (subtle shades of green), but hard to define precisely.

Let's leave the last four (more detailed) features for the moment and just consider the first two: basic leaf shape and leaf arrangement. There are two other basic shapes in addition to simple and lobed – first, a compound leaf such as that found in Rowan.

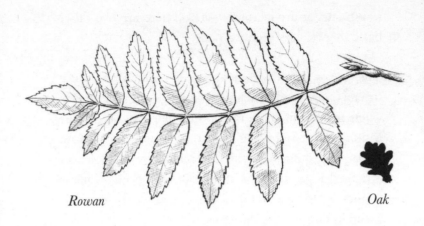

Rowan   *Oak*

Imagine that the lobes of the oak leaf are so deeply cut that the leaf was divided into a number of smaller segments, or leaflets. We can distinguish a compound leaf from a twig with opposite pairs of leaves by looking for buds. At the base of all leaves, immediately above their point of attachment with the stem (a position referred to as the axil of the leaf), there is a bud, destined to be a lateral bud (see species B). No such buds occur in the axils of any of the leaflets of a compound leaf (see Rowan leaf above). Similarly, at the tip of all twigs there is a terminal bud, whereas the midrib (large vein along the midline) of a compound leaf terminates with a leaflet.

The fourth basic shape is the needle. The leaves of conifers are not broad but long, thin and needle-like. We will discuss the differences between flowering plants and conifers on page 137.

Now you are ready to identify trees in just three steps.

THE THREE-STEP ID METHOD

The first step to identification by leaf, considers leaf shape (four types) and leaf arrangement (two types). This classifies the trees into eight categories, or boxes. Boxes help us to narrow the field when working out the identity of a 'new' tree.

We have 52 native trees. If they were to be distributed evenly between the eight boxes, there would be six or seven in each box. Suddenly, the identification challenge seems more manageable. Our two species now need to be distinguished between only the other members of their respective boxes.

Summary of Leaf Key 1

Basic leaf shape & arrangement	Alternate	Opposite
Simple	31 *(species A)*	7
Lobed	6	3 *(species B)*
Compound	1	2
Needle	2	1

However, if you look at the numbers in the boxes above (and at Leaf Key 1), you will see that most species fall into just one of these boxes. This means that the other boxes have correspondingly fewer species, making them even easier to sort. Species B, with its opposite, lobed leaves, is only one of three in its box and by comparing the three descriptions in the full version of this summary, Leaf Key 1, it should be simple to determine which species it is. (See footnote for the answer.[10]) Species A falls into the most popular box, along with 30 other species which all have simple alternate leaves. In order to distinguish it from all its bedfellows, you will need to move on to Step 2 by considering some new key features and referring to Leaf Key 2a. (Keys 2b and 2c cater for the species in the other two 'full' boxes – simple/opposite (seven species) and lobed/alternate (six species), respectively.)

Leaf Key 2a considers a new aspect of leaf shape – its length to width ratio, i.e. long and thin versus short and broad, in combination with features of the leaf margin (i.e. edge), is it entire or is it serrate in some way? These two features tend not to alter throughout the life of the leaf or age of the tree. Leaf size, though significant, is inevitably imprecise because leaf size varies within a range. And of course, there is considerable overlap of ranges between species, making 'size' a rather ill-defined feature. Hairiness is often referred to in the descriptions inside the boxes, but this feature does not work reliably for all species. Many start the season quite hairy, but by midsummer they are completely bald.

---

10   Species B is Field Maple.

We have defined the following:

Leaf Shape and Margin

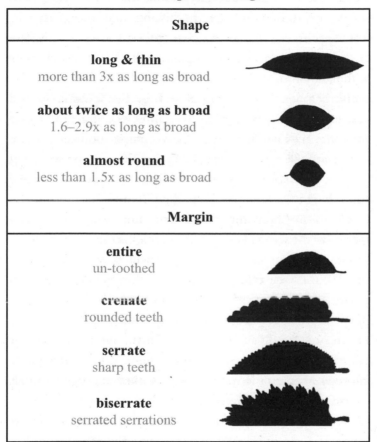

Shape
long & thin more than 3x as long as broad
about twice as long as broad 1.6–2.9x as long as broad
almost round less than 1.5x as long as broad
Margin
entire un-toothed
crenate rounded teeth
serrate sharp teeth
biserrate serrated serrations

Most of the trees with simple alternate leaves will 'key out' (be identifed) in Leaf Key 2a. But for some, including species A, which is almost round and has a serrate margin, you will need to progress to the third step. In this case that is Leaf Key 3a, which covers the six species that share these characteristics. Having compared the descriptions, check your conclusion with the footnote below.[11]

Remember that in using these Leaf Keys, you will never take more than three steps to name your tree. Although there are six Leaf Keys, you focus on only one key at each step. But take care to turn to the correct one! For species A we progressed from Leaf Key 1 to Key 2a (not 2b or 2c), and from there we were directed to 3a (not 3b).

If you are ever undecided, first check that you haven't turned to the wrong key, and then look for more information in the accounts of those species which share the same box. If the tree refuses to key out, it is probably a non-native species, but be wary of the lookalike alien species, particularly if you are tree-spotting in your garden or semi-urban surroundings. Often, confusing alien species are closely related to our native ones, such as Paper-bark Birch, Norway Maple or Turkey Oak, but even these are usually clearly distinct in some way.

This three-step method is not difficult and does not take long. And the more you use the keys, the more confident you will feel. Try it out with trees you already know. Until you become confident in tree recognition, don't ask a more knowledgeable friend or use an app – have a go at identifying

---

11 Species A is Downy Birch.

trees accurately by looking for specific key features with this three-step method. The process of identification is not nearly as challenging as many people imagine. And the benefit is that the process draws you closer to the tree; you discover first-hand the unique beauty of its finer detail, and this knowledge gives you a heightened sense of intimacy and respect. No app can give you that opportunity.

There is a ruler on page 304 for measuring the length and width of leaves.

ID Step 1 – What is the basic leaf shape and how are the leaves arranged?

Leaf Outline	Alternate	Opposite (or whorls of 3)
Simple	**Thirty-one Species** Go to **Leaf Key 2a**	**Seven Species** Go to **Leaf Key 2b**
Lobed	**Six Species** Go to **Leaf Key 2c**	entire margin, heart-shaped base — **Field Maple** p. 246 (2); serrated margin, heart-shaped base — **Sycamore** p. 246 (5); serrated margin, rounded base — **Guelder-rose** p. 273 (4)
Compound	11–19 leaflets — **Rowan** p. 194 (6)	9–13 leaflets — **Ash** p. 265 (1); 5–7 leaflets — **Elder** p. 273 (3)
Needle	single needles — **Yew** p. 147 (9); needles in pairs — **Scots Pine** p. 141 (8)	spiky needles in whorls of 3 — **Juniper** p. 144 (7)

Leaf Key 1

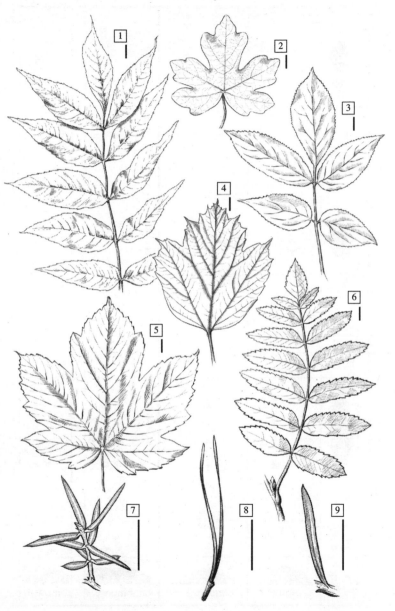

Leaf Key 2a: Alternate Simple Leaves

ID Step 2 – What are the leaf proportions and is the leaf margin toothed?

Leaf Margin	Proportion > 3x	Proportion ~2x	Proportion <1.5x
Entire	plant not spiny — **Osier 6** p. 166 plant very spiny — **Sea Buckthorn 2** p. 203	shiny evergreen (some have a spiky, lobed margin) — **Holly 4** p. 270	undulating hairy margin — **Beech 5** p. 219 often almost in opposite pairs — **Alder Buckthorn 11** p. 200
Crenate	evergreen — **Strawberry Tree 3** p. 260	deciduous — **Three Willow Species Goat, Grey & Bay** *see Willows* p. 166 evergreen (some ~2x as long as wide) — **Strawberry Tree 3** p. 260 *most >3x long as wide*	flattened petiole — **Aspen 1** p. 161 undulating hairy margin — **Beech 5** p. 219
Serrate	serrations only at vein ends — **Sweet Chestnut 8** p. 223 fine even serrations — **Three Willow Species Crack, Almond & White** *see Willows* p. 166	spiny twigs — **Blackthorn 10** p. 181 2 small red glands at top of petiole — **Two Cherries Wild & Bird 9,7** *see Cherries* p. 181	**Six species** Go to **Leaf Key 3a**
Biserrate		**Four Species** Go to **Leaf Key 3b**	**Five Species** Go to **Leaf Key 3b**

Leaf Key 2a

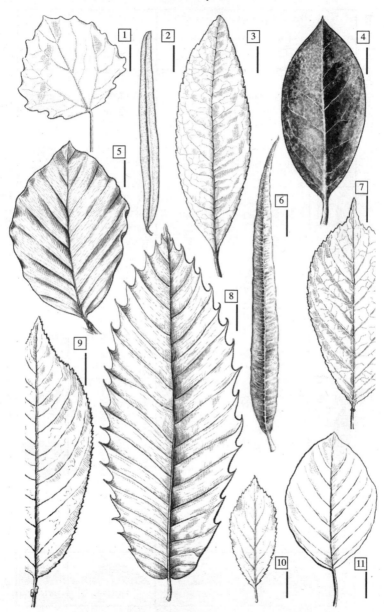

Leaf Key 2b: Opposite, Simple Leaves

ID Step 2 – Is the leaf margin serrated or entire?

Serrate leaf margin	<1.5 x	hairless except stalk; often not quite opposite	**Buckthorn** p. 200
	~ 2 x	veins reach the margin; very hairy, star-shaped hairs	**Wayfaring Tree** p. 273
	>3 x	serrated only towards the tip	**Purple Willow** p. 176
	~ 2 x	obscure serrations; green twigs	**Spindle** p. 154
Entire leaf margin	~2 x	veins don't reach margin; twigs often red	**Dogwood** p. 257
	~2 x	semi evergreen; pointed tip	**Privet** p. 263
	~2 x	evergreen; round or notched at tip	**Box** p. 151

NB Purple Willow & Spindle can look entire – see Serrate leaf margin above and use a hand lens

Leaf Key 2b

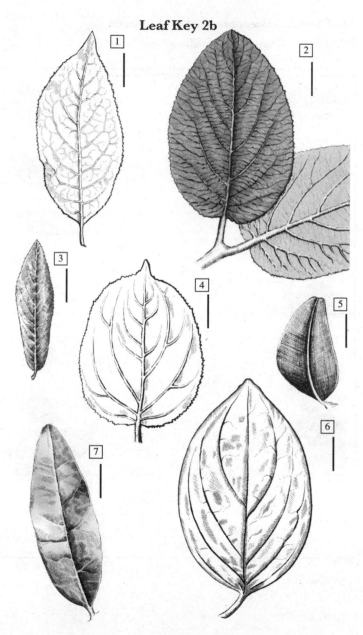

Leaf Key 2c: Alternate, Lobed Leaves

ID Step 2 – What shape are the lobes?

	evergreen & spiny (some are entire & spineless)	**Holly** p. 270
	acutely lobed; lobes <½ way to midrib; hairy underside	**Wild Service Tree** p. 194
	deeply cut, acute lobes	**Hawthorn** p. 190
	(intermediates occur)	(Hybrid thorn)
	three shallow, rounded lobes	**Midland Thorn** p. 190
	Stalk <5mm; leaf blade forms auricles	**Pedunculate Oak** p. 227
	(intermediates occur)	(Hybrid oak)
	Stalk >10mm; cuneate base to leaf blade	**Sessile Oak** p. 227

Leaf Key 2c

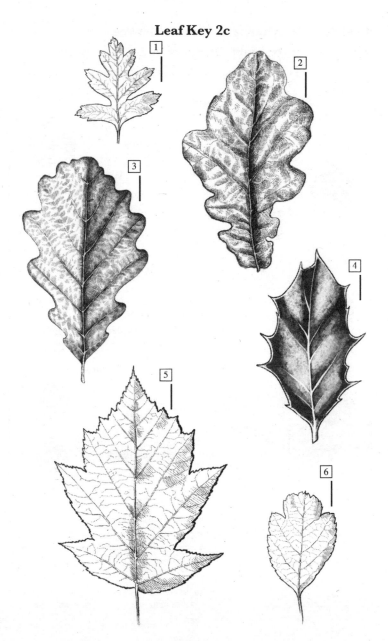

Leaf Key 3a: Alternate, Simple Leaves, with Simply Serrate Margins <1.5x as Long as Wide
ID Step 3 – Is the leaf symmetrical or lopsided?

Lopsided	6–10cm long; sparsely hairy on lower surface	**Large-leaved Lime** p. 252	
	6–10cm long; white hair tufts on lower surface	**Lime** p. 252	
	3–7cm long; orange hair tufts on lower surface	**Small-leaved Lime** p. 252	1
Symmetrical	ace of spades shape	**Black Poplar** p. 161	3
	stout hairy twigs with concertinaed wrinkles	**Crab Apple** p. 186	4
	slender hairy twigs	**Downy Birch** p. 233	2

Leaf Key 3a

Leaf Key 3b: Alternate Simple Leaves with Biserrate Margins

ID Step 3 – What are the leaf proportions?

<1.5x as long as wide	asymmetrical base; roughly hairy	**English Elm** p. 208	
	indented leaf tip	**Alder** p. 238	
	white, felty underside; often ~2x long as wide	**Whitebeam** p. 194	
	long pointed tip; heart-shaped base	**Hazel** p. 241	
	ace of spades shape; shiny, warty twigs	**Silver Birch** p. 233	
~2x as long as wide	asymmetrical base; roughly hairy	**Wych Elm** p. 208	
	asymmetrical base; upper surface hairless	**Field Elm** p. 208	
	pleated look	**Hornbeam** p. 244	
	white, felty underside; also often <1.5x long as wide	**Whitebeam** p. 194	

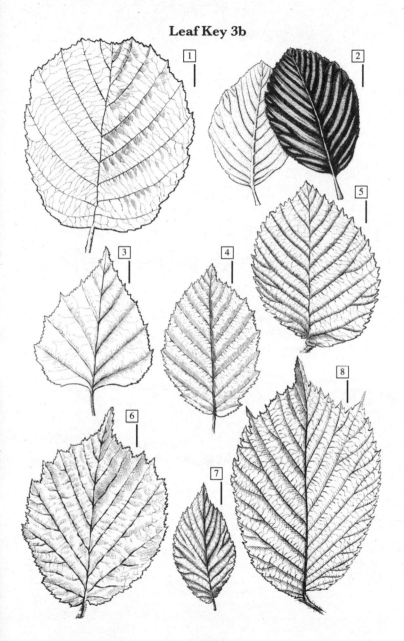

8

Identifying Trees in Winter: Using Twigs and Buds

AWAITING SPRING

IDENTIFYING PLANTS IS not rocket science, though occasionally it does require lots of patience and a good hand lens. Identifying trees in winter is one of those occasions.

Most of our trees are deciduous – they lose their leaves during autumn and grow fresh shoots and leaves in the spring. This feature, one we take for granted, is characteristic only of those trees that belong to cool, temperate regions. To people from other climes, who are unaccustomed to this phenomenon, our trees look dead during the winter. But they are not dead; they are behaving tactically and patiently – awaiting spring.

DECIDUOUS VERSUS EVERGREEN

Most trees of the tropical rainforests and of the cold boreal coniferous forests are evergreen. The deciduous trees of temperate zones lose their leaves to conserve water and to help them survive stormy winter weather conditions. Such tactics are unnecessary in the tropics, and in Arctic and Boreal locations, summers are too short for plants to spend time regrowing leaves.

Because deciduous trees are without the weight and wind resistance of leaves during the winter months, they experience much less branch and trunk breakage from storms and the weight of snow. The delicate tissues of soft leaves are neither shredded nor crushed by ice formation. Despite precipitation often being greater in the winter, the availability of liquid water is reduced when the temperature drops. No leaves means much less need for water and much less water loss. Regrowing leaves in the spring is cheaper on resources than keeping them functioning and repaired through the winter.

Plants that remain green throughout the winter are likely to suffer greater water loss, a pounding from winter storms and greater browsing pressure, particularly since there's not much other food about at this time of year. So their leaves are equipped with at least one of these resilient and defensive features: a tough, waxy cuticle, spiky margins, a bitter taste and toxicity if consumed. Consider Holly and the tough resinous needles of Scots Pine and Juniper. Many tropical species already exhibit some of these features. The deciduous habit is a strategy that evolved relatively recently.

In the absence of leaves, we are denied the most familiar and easiest of tree ID features. We have already considered that using the silhouette of the tree and characteristics of the bark have major limitations, so now all we can turn to are the twigs, and especially their buds.

BUDS

A bud is a miraculous feature – a tiny, dormant blob, within which is contained the potential to produce a substantial shoot, sometimes over a metre long, and thick with leaves. Alternatively, some burst open to reveal a beautiful spray of flowers, a catkin or maybe just a single immaculate bloom. All this is tied up in a minute, nondescript package.

Buds (whether flower buds or vegetative buds) always occur immediately above the point where the leaf is attached to the twig. Here, like the leaf, it is nourished from a branch of the main vascular system, and the leaf provides the bud with protection during its early development the previous summer. When the leaf drops, a scar remains on the twig, immediately below the bud. If you look closely at the scar, you can see the veins that fed the leaf via its stalk, and which carried sugars from the leaf to other parts of the plant. The number of veins depends on the species. These veins become plugged by cork prior to leaf fall, to prevent infection of the wound. Sometimes their location is made more obvious by minute pimples of cork. The shape of the leaf scar and the number of vein scars can be used in identification, but we are not using that feature in this book.

Twig Anatomy

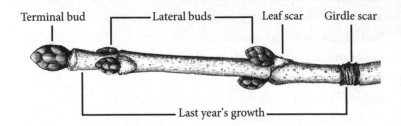

Terminal bud — Lateral buds — Leaf scar — Girdle scar

Last year's growth

Girdle scars also occur around the twig. These represent the scars left by the bud scales (see below) of the terminal bud when it burst the previous spring. The length of twig between the girdle scars indicates the amount of growth during that season.

When we identify trees by their leaves, one of the main features is to consider how they are arranged on the twigs. So it is with the buds. If the leaves are in opposite pairs, the associated buds will be opposite. And if the buds are opposite, so will their shoots and ultimately the branches be opposite. That first step in identifying a tree can often be simply looking up into the leafless canopy and observing how the smaller branches are arranged. Bear in mind, though, that twigs break off for all sorts of reasons, so not every twig or branch will retain an opposite number.

Unless you can recognise the tree in winter by a collection of often intangible features, you will need to observe the buds closely to progress further with the identification process. Some of the details of the buds are exquisite. The main features to check are the surface of the bud, its shape, alignment, colour and hairiness.

Almost all buds are tightly packed inside a number of bud scales which are derived from leaves – though modified and greatly reduced in size. Most trees have more than three bud scales per bud, sometimes many more. It isn't always necessary to count them, just to establish that there are more than three (>3). Even buds that are less than 2mm in size may have more than three scales. You need a lens!

The buds of some trees are equipped with only two or three or – in the case of willows (and only willows) – only one bud scale. The buds of some species are not protected by scales; what you see are the first tiny, folded and dormant immature leaves of the shoot that will develop fully come the spring. Beginners find it tricky to work out if they are looking at scales or immature leaves. Scales are smoother, with no gaps between them. Note that there are only three species without bud scales, and one of those has alternate buds, while the other two have opposite.

The shape of the bud is useful. 'Spindle shaped' are long and thin. 'Rounded' are generally broader and shorter; these are usually blunt, but they may be pointed. Many buds that are attached to the side of the twig (lateral buds) are pressed against it – appressed – while others stick out more obviously – prominent. The lateral buds of trees tend to be consistently appressed or consistently prominent. But sometimes they may appear intermediate, which is irritating, as this is generally a useful key feature.

Number of Bud Scales

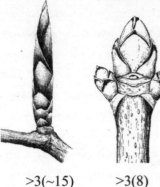

>3(~15) >3(8) 2 0

Most twigs become shades of brown or grey during their first year, so it is unusual to find buds attached to green twigs the following winter. However, buds can be various shades of green, brown, black, yellow or red. The colour of the bud as well as the twig is usually characteristic, but the twigs and buds of many species will flush pink or red when they are exposed to the sun. This is more obvious in the winter when the leaves are off the tree, at the edge of a wood or the sunny side of a hedge. It is almost as though the twig becomes sunburnt, but actually, it's quite the opposite – the red pigment increases to protect the inner tissues from damaging UV rays. So be prepared to be flexible when assessing colour.

Another variable feature is hairiness, which is usually visible only with a hand lens. Many species, whose buds and twigs are thickly coated in hairs at the start of winter, end up with bald versions of both by the end. Therefore, this feature is used sparingly in the keys, and you should be conscious of the month when you are tackling an ID. Buds are easier to study towards the end of winter, when they are at their largest and beginning to swell – but don't leave it too late. And you will definitely need a lens.

Buds are tricky – use other clues to verify your hunches where you can. Search for persistent fruits and leaves. But be wary of fallen leaves – they may have blown in.

Since evergreen species can be identified more simply by their leaves, we have omitted them from these keys. These include Holly, Box, Strawberry Tree and our three conifers – Scots Pine, Juniper and Yew.

TWIG IDENTIFICATION KEYS

First decide which Key to turn to when identifying an 'unknown' species. (There is a ruler on page 304.)

1. How are the buds arranged?

Opposite buds   ⟶ Turn to **Key 1** (p. 122)

Alternate/spirally

arranged   ⟶ Go to question 2

2. How many bud scales are there?

– 0–3 (or rarely, 4)   ⟶ Turn to **Key 2** (p. 125)

– >3 bud scales   ⟶ Go to question 3

3. Are some of the buds clustered?

– Yes   ⟶ Turn to **Key 3a** (p. 126)

– No – for buds that are

slender and pointed ⟶ Turn to **Key 3b** (p. 126)

– No – for buds that

are rounded   ⟶ Turn to **Key 4** (p. 128)

Twig Key 1: Opposite Buds

The first division here is whether the two buds in a pair are 'connected' or free. Those that are connected have leaf scars that are linked by a faint straight or V-shaped line or a ridge and tend to be strictly opposite. Look carefully. The two buds in a pair that are free, i.e. not connected in this way, often fall out of line and become sub-opposite.

Another feature that is mentioned is a corky-ridged twig. For an illustration see page 212.

ID Step 1 – Are the buds connected?
  – How many bud scales are there?

	Buds Connected		Buds Free	
0 **Bud** **Scales**	Buds & twigs red (at least tinged)	**Dogwood** p. 257 **11**		
	Buds brown; twigs pale brown & hairy; terminal bud like a horned Viking helmet	**Wayfaring Tree** p. 273 **7**		
1–3 **Bud** **Scales**	Buds red; twigs angled in cross-section	**Guelder-rose** p. 273 **6**	Buds black	**Ash** p. 265 **1**
			Buds red-purple, appressed; 1 bud scale	**Purple Willow** p. 166 **2**
>3 **Bud** **Scales**	Dark purple buds that burst early (ragged); twigs pale brown & warty	**Elder** p. 273 **10**	Buds 2mm, green to red; twigs grey, narrow & hairless	**Wild Privet** p. 263 **4**
	Pale brown, hairy buds, <4mm; 2+ year-old twigs often develop corky ridges	**Field Maple** p. 246 **9**	Green twigs & buds; twigs remain green for 3 years when they often develop corky ridges	**Spindle** p. 154 **3**
	Green bud scales with dark margins; stout, terminal bud	**Sycamore** p. 246 **8**	Buds dark brown, terminal buds often replaced by short spines	**Buckthorn** p. 200 **5**

Twig Key 1

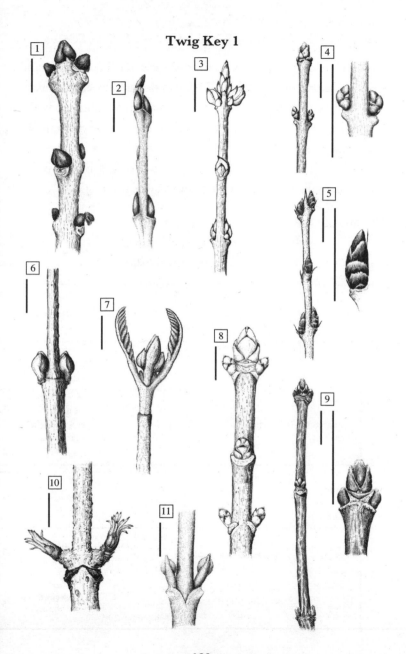

Twig Key 2: Alternate Buds with 0–3(4) Bud Scales

Willows, and only willows, can be spotted easily by their single bud scale. However willow ID between species can be very tricky during winter.

Generally, when judging leaf and bud arrangement, 'alternate' is considered to be synonymous with 'spiral'. However, in this key we ask you to distinguish between the two. A strictly alternate arrangement appears to zigzag.

ID Step 2 – How many bud scales?
   – Are the buds spiral or alternate?
   – Are the buds slender or plump?

0 Bud Scales		Very hairy brown buds without scales; brown twigs, hairy only towards tip	**Alder Buckthorn** p. 200	1
1 Bud Scales	buds spiral slender appressed	Hairy buds & twigs	**Osier, White & Grey Willows** p. 166	3
		Hairless buds & twigs	**Crack, Almond & Bay Willows** p. 166	
	buds spiral plump prominent	Buds yellow, turning brown	**Goat Willows** p. 166	2
2 Bud Scales	buds spiral plump prominent	Buds 7–10mm, dull purple all on individual bud stalks; woody cones present on mature trees	**Alder** p. 238	4
		Buds 3–6mm, brown, often oblique above leaf scars; sometimes alternate; ridged twigs	**Sweet Chestnut** p. 223	5

2–3(4) Bud Scales	buds alternate plump prominent	Buds 3–6mm, brown, often oblique above leaf scars; buds sometimes spiral; ridged twigs	**Sweet Chestnut** p. 223	**5**
		Buds <4(–6)mm, scales 2(3), buds & hairless twigs mostly red, greenish when growing in shade	**Small-leaved Lime** p. 252	**6**
		Buds 6–9mm, scales 3(4), buds & hairy twigs mostly green, tinged red when growing in sun	**Large-leaved Lime** p. 252	
		Buds 6–9mm, scales 3(4); intermediate features; lots of epicormic growth	**Lime** p. 252	

Twig Key 2

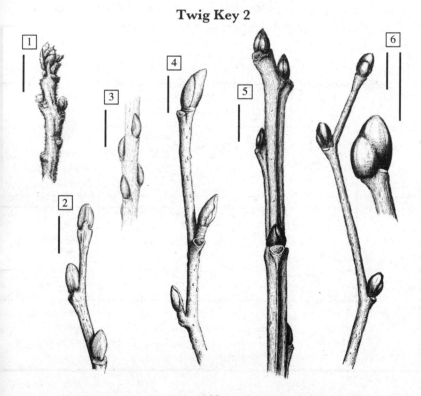

Twig Key 3 (and 4): Alternate Buds with >3 Bud Scales

Twig Key 3a: Buds Clustered

ID Step 3a – Where are the buds clustered?

Buds clustered at tips of leading shoots	Blunt buds <20 bud scales	**Pedunculate Oak** p. 227	8
	Pointed buds >20 bud scales	**Sessile Oak** p. 227	9
Buds clustered at tips of short side shoots	Horizontal cracks in trunk bark	**Wild Cherry** p. 181	4

Twig Key 3b: Buds Slender and Pointed (not Clustered)

Sometimes trees with appressed buds also bear terminal buds at the tips of very short side shoots. Because these are more obvious than the appressed lateral buds they appear as prominent laterals. Look carefully.

Remember that an appressed lateral bud might sometimes seem prominent and vice versa. Look at several.

ID Step 3b – Are the buds appressed or prominent?

Buds appressed & sticky	Buds 7mm hairless & glossy		**Aspen** p. 161	1
	Buds 7mm, hairless, tips usually arch outwards		**Black Poplar** p. 161	3
Buds prominent	Buds 15–20mm, spindle-shaped straight, long, brown & stick out		**Beech** p. 219	2
	Buds 6–8 mm, often curved close to twig; 6 brown bud scales sometimes green at base		**Hornbeam** p. 244	7
	Buds 6–8 mm, straight, forward-pointing; bud scales dark with pale edges		**Bird Cherry** p. 181	6
	Buds 6mm, pointed Catkins usually present (both immature ♂, often in pairs at twig tips, and fruiting ♀)	Hairless twigs with pale warts	**Silver Birch** p. 233	5
		Downy twigs with no warts	**Downy Birch** p. 233	

Twig Key 3

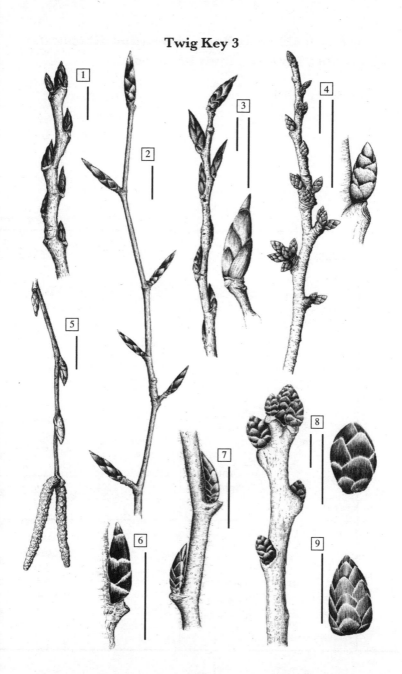

Twig Key 4: Alternate Buds with >3 Bud Scales (Buds Not Clustered); Buds Rounded

Hairiness in this key is reasonably consistent regardless of season, but it is tricky to discern the number of bud scales when they are covered with hairs, particularly when the buds are very small.

ID Step 4 – Are the buds hairy or hairless?
      – How large are the buds?

		Buds <5mm		Buds >5mm	
Hairy Buds	Buds 1–2 mm; short, side shoots often end in thorns	**Blackthorn** p. 181	1	Buds 7 mm pinched/ slightly flattened in one plane; scales green (reddish) with hairy margins; downy twigs	**Hazel** p. 241	2
	Buds 2–4 mm; twigs sparsely hairy	**Field Elm** p. 208		Buds 7–10 mm acute; not central to leaf scar; orange hairs on twigs	**Wych Elm** p. 208	3
	Buds 2–4 mm; twigs hairy, often corky-ridged	**English Elm** p. 208	7	Buds 7–10 mm acute; bud scales hairy-edged, green	**Whitebeam** p. 194	5
	Buds 2–5 mm; hairy-tipped; short side shoots; wrinkled twigs	**Crab Apple** p. 186	4	Buds >15mm, acute; bud scales hairy all over, dark red-brown	**Rowan** p. 194	9
Hairless Buds	Buds 3–4 mm; hairless, thorny twigs; usually 1 nut per haw	**Hawthorn** p. 190	6	Buds round, 5–6mm; scales green with dark (often frayed) borders; twigs hairy towards tip	**Wild Service Tree** p. 194	8
	Buds 3–4 mm; hairless twigs, less thorny; usually 2 nuts per haw	**Midland Hawthorn** p. 190				

Twig Key 4

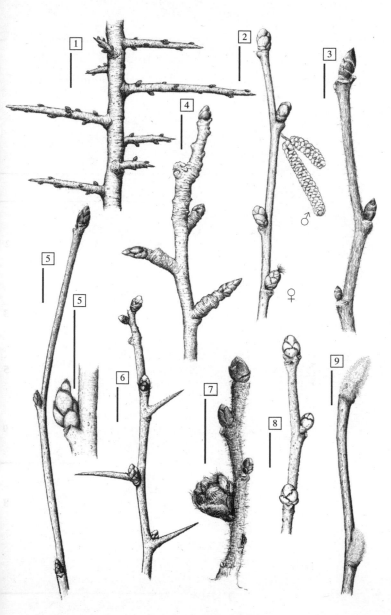

PART THREE

SPECIES
PROFILES

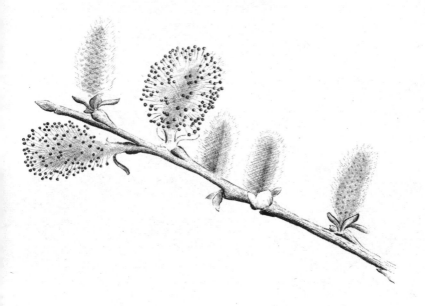

9

Britain's 52 (Mostly) Native Trees

HOW DID WE SELECT THEM?

PART THREE OF this book focuses on each of our selected species. More than 1,500 different species of trees grow in Britain today – far too many to cover in a book of this size. So we needed to adopt some selection criteria.

We decided to focus primarily on the native species (those that migrated back before the Channel flooded) plus a few of those that were introduced by early humans, including the four narrow-leaved willows. Such species have been around almost as long as the natives and are called archaeophytes. We also selected just two of the many species that have been introduced much more recently and have become almost as common as the natives, or more so. Species that joined our flora after 1492, the year Christopher Columbus first made contact with the Americas, are called neophytes. (Note that not all neophytes originated in the Americas, though many did.) Sycamore is a neophyte but Sweet Chestnut was introduced around 1100, so technically it is still an archaeophyte. Both originated in mainland Europe.

We first thought we would look only at trees, not shrubs. But there is a continuum and lots of overlap with no clear cut-off point. Shrubs range in stature from robust and tall (more than 15 metres) to prostrate and growing horizontally. We decided to accept both trees and shrubs, so long as they were able to grow over 4 metres in height.

HOW WE HAVE ARRANGED THEM

We settled on a way of arranging them that reflects their filial relationship best, so that species with similar features are grouped together. This is the approach that taxonomists use to classify plants. We adopted the APG system outlined on page 36. Classification systems continually evolve in response to ongoing research; as a result, some older books may organise their trees in a slightly different sequence.

For the larger families, which contain several species, we start with some general family characteristics before exploring the individual species.

10

The Conifers

FOR ALMOST 200 million years, from the Triassic through the Age of the Dinosaurs (the Jurassic) to the Cretaceous period, conifers were the dominant plants across the Earth's land surface. But during the Cretaceous (145–66 million years ago), they were superseded by the flowering plants. Many conifers became extinct, leaving only 630 species, and of those that remain, several retain only a tenuous toehold in very restricted locations in the world.

GEOLOGICAL TIMELINE

Era	Million years ago (mya)	Period	Plant life
Cenozoic	2.6	Quaternary	Ice Age obliterates all forests in the BI
	66	Tertiary	Laurisilva in Europe incl BI
Mesozoic	145	Cretaceous	Flowering plants expand
	201	Jurassic	Flowering plants appear 175 mya
	252	Triassic	Conifers appeared 300 mya

Four hundred of those 630 species live in the northern hemisphere, where some still dominate the forests that extend across the vast, cold, damp landscapes that span the Temperate and Arctic regions. With the seemingly unstoppable destruction of the tropical rainforests, these coniferous boreal forests are becoming proportionately more significant in their role as critical carbon sinks. The efficacy of conifers in this respect can be attributed to the great longevity of the live evergreen needles and their characteristically slow rate of decay after falling – and also, in the case of the largest family, the Pinaceae, to the essential ectomycorrhizal partnerships that not only enable the trees to survive but also dramatically enhance their growth rates on inhospitable soils.

THE DIFFERENCE BETWEEN CONIFERS AND FLOWERING PLANTS

There are many different ways of defining each of the major groups of plants – mosses, liverworts, ferns, horsetails, conifers, flowering plants, etc. But most of them prove inadequate for distinguishing conclusively between them. Early botanists shrewdly focused on the reproductive organs and strategies, recognising that these closely reflected their evolutionary relationships. This turned out to be a sound and reliable base for a taxonomic classification and recent advances in genetic analysis have confirmed that the wisdom of those early botanists could substantially stand the test of time.

An understanding of the reproductive strategies and features of the conifers and the broad-leaved trees helps provide an insight into the classification of not only these groups but also of the family subgroups within them.

The plant kingdom can be split roughly into those that reproduce by spores (the mosses and ferns and their allies) and those that reproduce by seeds. The seed plants are divided into the conifers (not all of which bear cones) and the flowering plants. Nearly all the trees on the planet bear seeds – 630 conifers and 50,435 flowering or broad-leaved trees (a ratio of roughly 1:80).[12] In Britain we have three native conifers and 51 flowering or broad-leaved trees. So although three is not many, in the British context it exceeds the global ratio.

The label 'conifers' obviously refers to most members of the group which produce cones. These are the female structures of the tree, in which reproduction takes place and the resulting seeds mature before dispersal. Conifers are predominantly evergreen trees. Most contain resin, have needle- or scale-like leaves, are monoecious, and bear woody cones; all are wind-pollinated. However, none of these features is exclusive to conifers, and many flowering plants, even those in northern temperate regions, may have one or other of these qualities.

A more satisfactory distinguishing feature can be summed up in the scientific name for the conifers (plus Ginkgo and the cycads) – the gymnosperms, literally 'naked seeds' (from the Greek *gymno*, meaning 'naked', as in gymnasium, and *sperma*, meaning 'seed'). The seeds of conifers lie naked on the upper surface of the cone scales, while the seeds of flowering plants are embedded inside a fruit – their scientific name is angiosperms (from the Greek *angio*, meaning 'a vessel' and *sperma*, again meaning 'seed').

More accurately, these names (gymnosperms and angiosperms) refer not to the seeds but the precursors of the seeds – the ovules. In gymnosperms, such as Scots Pine, the ovules (which contain the female gametes) lie naked on the surface of

---

12   Gatti RC et al. (2022). The number of tree species on Earth. Proceedings of the National Academy of Sciences. doi.org/10.1073/pnas.2115329119

Male 'cones'   Immature female cones   Mature female cones

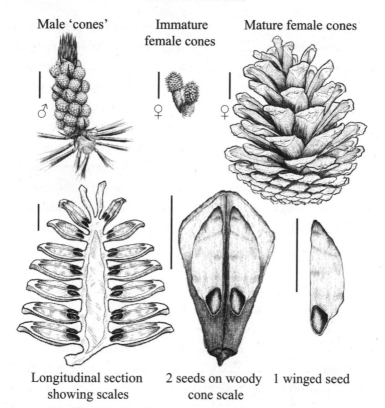

Longitudinal section showing scales   2 seeds on woody cone scale   1 winged seed

the immature scales of the tiny, freshly opened female cones, which at this stage are soft, with scales not tightly clasped together. Pollen is produced by pollen sacks – analogous to the stamens of flowering plants, which are bunched together in clusters, with several clusters making up a temporary, soft male 'cone'. (Both male and female cones are generally found on the same tree, though the male cones are shed once the pollen is released.)

Each grain of pollen carries a male gamete and drifts in the wind or is simply carried on air currents through the canopy.

The pollen floats between the branches, twigs and needles – and between the female cone scales. Some of the pollen (from the same or different trees) will lodge directly on the surface of the ovules, and ultimately, fertilisation takes place. In other words, the male and female gametes (if compatible) combine to form a zygote that develops into the seed. Once the ovules in a cone have been fertilised, the scales close together to protect the developing seeds while they mature. Over the following year (or two), the scales and the whole cone become more robust and increase in size and when the time is right the now woody scales gape open again to release the winged seeds to be dispersed on the wind.

Compare this with the process of pollination and fruit development in the broad-leaved trees which are flowering plants (angiosperms).

In Britain we have one native example from each of the three conifer families that are found mostly in the northern hemisphere. Two of the three, Juniper and Yew, are exceptions to the 'typical conifer' in more ways than one. In both cases, each individual tree is dioecious (either male or female (dioecious means two homes, a home (tree) for the male and another home for the female). Also, while the male trees produce small and short-lived pollen cones typical of other conifers, the female trees of both species produce berry-like 'cones' rather than the typical woody cones of most conifers.

Many different conifers from all over the world have been introduced to the British Isles and planted in parks and gardens. Others are grown commercially in forestry plant-ations. About 40 species have managed to establish themselves in the wild, but not in any abundance. Nevertheless, do not presume that a conifer growing in a natural habitat must be one of our three natives. Be aware of non-natives. In the absence of cones and 'berries', you'll need to check the foliage. Remember: even if it is the cone season, male specimens of Juniper and Yew will never bear 'berries', though they will have had short-lived male 'cones' to produce the pollen.

PINACEAE

Scots Pine *Pinus sylvestris*

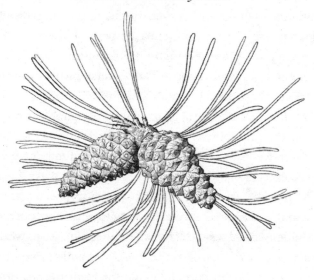

The Caledonian pine forests of the western and central Highlands of Scotland are a magical taste of the wonderful natural forest that once clad most of the Scottish Highlands. The trees are generally well-spaced, blending seamlessly into the open, heather-clad moorland and allowing magnificent vistas across a dramatic landscape.

Tree-spotting

Although it was not one of the pioneers, Scots Pine colonised Britain very early on, entering the south via northern France and spreading northwards up the Atlantic seaboard – and also entering the east coast from Scandinavia via Doggerland. Its dominance in the south and west diminished with the spread of mixed oak forest during the warm Atlantic period, around 5000 BP, and again as a result of over-exploitation by humans. But it survived as the dominant species on the poor, acid soils of Scotland and the north of England until the twentieth century. Now, its truly natural distribution in Britain is restricted to remnants of the Caledonian pine forest. But it can be found, often planted alongside other pines, throughout the country.

Pinus is the largest genus of all conifers, with 113 species. Pines occur in a huge range of habitats from cold and wet to hot and dry, with the greatest diversity in Mexico. Scots Pine is the only pine native to northern Europe. It occurs throughout Europe, except the south, and stretches in a narrow band as far as eastern Asia.

The needles of nearly all pine species are bound together in pairs, groups of three or groups of five, depending on the species. They are attached to tiny stumps that are spirally arranged around the twig. As with all evergreen conifers, the needles do not fall all together at the same time in the autumn, but randomly throughout the year, and are regularly replaced. Pine needles can last several years before they fall (which they do, still attached in their group of two, three or five).

Scots Pine is a two-needled pine that can grow to 36 metres. The needles are relatively short for pines – between 2–8cm long.

Scots Pine

They are bluey-green and each one is twisted. The bark of a mature tree is a warm pinky-orange, especially towards the top of the tree.

All 113 pine species bear cones, as do all members of the family Pinaceae, which also includes firs, spruces, larches and cedars. In common with most conifers and also most of our broad-leaved trees, but unlike Yew and Juniper, all pines are monoecious – both female cones and the short-lived male cones occur on the same tree (one home – one tree – for both sexes). Like the needles, the mature cones of Scots Pine, between 2.5–7.5cm long, are relatively short for pines.

CUPRESSACEAE

Juniper *Juniperus communis*

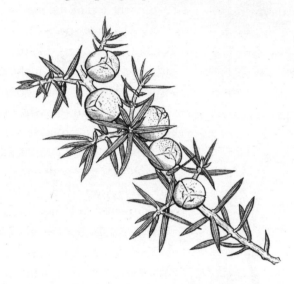

Our native Juniper is the world's most widespread conifer species. In its dwarf form, it was one of the pioneers of the early tundra landscape at the end of the Ice Age. In Britain today, Juniper exists as three subspecies – ssp. *communis* grows as a low-growing shrub in the north and west, and as a taller (though rare) shrub or tree (up to 10 metres high) on the chalk downs of southern England. Ssp. *nana* is always prostrate and grows in the extreme northwest of Britain and Ireland. (The third, ssp. *hemisphaerica*, is extremely rare, prostrate and confined to maritime cliffs in west Cornwall.) All forms are light-demanding plants. Sadly, the future doesn't look good for the southern Juniper in particular. Numbers are declining. Excessive grazing prevents seedling development.

But the absence of grazing results in scrub and ultimately canopy development, which casts too much shade. It is a delicate tightrope to walk for those working to manage its survival. An additional threat to all the subspecies comes from a deadly fungus-like pathogen *Phytophthora austrocedri* that is sweeping the British Isles.

Our species retains its immature spiky foliage through to maturity. (Many other Junipers soon acquire small, overlapping, scale-like leaves similar to those of cypresses.) The stiff needles are sharply pointed, equidistantly placed around the twig in whorls of three, and are between 1 and 2cm long. They have a strong white band on the upper surface and they emit an unmistakable aroma when crushed.

Juniper

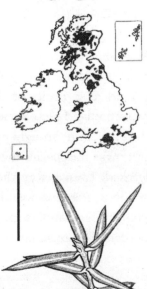

Most Cupressaceae (which includes cypresses and redwoods) bear round, woody cones. But each of the three scales of Juniper cones becomes succulent rather than woody and after fertilisation they fuse together, forming a dark purple berry about 1cm across. The three seeds remain embedded in the berry at dispersal.

All parts of Juniper, including the berries, release characteristic volatile aromatic oils – which are rich in monoterpenes – to protect the plant from bacterial attack.

The berries have long been used to help relieve stomach upsets caused by bacteria. In addition, the berries are a good source of vitamin C, and the monoterpenes have also been shown to provide anti-inflammatory and antioxidant properties. But the berries are unpalatable and bitter on their own. To make them more acceptable, in 1550, a Dutch doctor concocted a mix of Juniper berries with an alcoholic spirit, and the popular liquor gin (or genever) was born. Today there are over 6,000 different gins world-wide, each with its own unique flavour derived from a vast range of 'botanicals'. Common to all of them is the international regulatory requirement that the spirit contain Juniper as its base flavour. It is the only botanical present in all gins. Juniper berries impart the essential traditional pine-y, resin-y taste.

In the seventeenth century, British soldiers fighting in the Netherlands drank the spirit – not for medicinal purposes (though that excuse may often be used as a justification today) but to calm their nerves prior to battle. The soldiers acquired a liking for this Dutch courage and brought it back to England. Our common Juniper was the species that was and is still the most commonly used. Even before the extensive manufacture of gin in London in the seventeenth century, Juniper berries were gathered by highlanders and sold at markets in Inverness and Aberdeen before shipment to the Netherlands.

TAXACEAE

Yew *Taxus baccata*

Some of the most famous Yew forests of Europe occur on the steep scarp slopes of the chalk downs of southern England. It grows elsewhere in Britain but becomes increasingly less common in the colder north. Our Yew is the only species in its family (Taxaceae) to grow wild in Europe, where it is widespread and a survivor of the subtropical laurisilva forests of the Tertiary period.

A mature Yew develops a massive trunk, although the height seldom exceeds 25 metres. Unlike Juniper, the needles (1–3cm long) are soft, flexible and dark green and shiny on the upper side. The lower sides are a paler green and dull. They are attached spirally around the twig, though they often twist at the base so as to lie flat in one plane on either side. Yew leaves (like those of all Taxaceae) do not emit the unmistakable resin smell so characteristic of other conifers, even when they are crushed.

All members of the Taxaceae produce a unique type of 'berry'. The ovule sits in a thin green cup called an aril. After fertilisation the aril swells, becoming fleshy and mucilaginous but never completely enveloping the seed. Unlike the rest of the Yew tree, the aril does not contain toxins – but to ensure seed dispersal, it is bright red, sickly sweet, rich in energy and irresistible to birds. The seed is poisonous but passes undigested through the bird's gut.

Yew

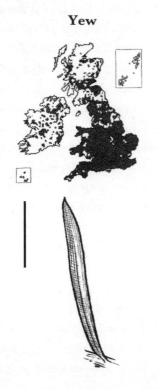

I have vivid memories of walking through a Suffolk churchyard at dusk one beastly cold December evening in the 1970s. There was a deafening racket coming from the ancient Yew trees, where hundreds of thrushes, Redwings and Fieldfares were noisily 'chacking' over a feast of yew 'berries' before darkness fell. And there they spent the night, sheltered from the bitter cold by the closeness of their neighbours and the dense cover of the evergreen branches.

Yews are often associated with churchyards. Over the years, farmers with livestock eliminated most Yews on their land because of the tree's toxicity, so churchyards became their haven. Yew's main toxic chemicals are terpene alkaloids called taxines that are strong cardiotoxins, and are therefore highly effective anti-browsing chemicals. Animals can build up immunity if fed small but increasing quantities, but they would normally avoid Yew unless they are extremely hungry.

Another type of toxin found in Yew are diterpenes, one of which is paclitaxel. It was first discovered in the Pacific Yew and is used to create a powerful chemotherapy drug. Note that it is lethally toxic unless administered in medically controlled quantities. Although our Yew does not contain paclitaxel, the leaves do contain a related compound that can be extracted and converted into paclitaxel. When I walked back through that Suffolk churchyard the following morning, I remember talking to the churchwarden, who told me that they would be gathering the Yew clippings the following summer to send to the nearest paclitaxel drug manufacturers. Artificial synthesis of paclitaxel has probably saved the Pacific Yew from over-exploitation.

11

Broad-leaved Trees

BUXACEAE

Box *Buxus sempervirens*

The extraordinary art of topiary – the transformation of trees and shrubs into geometric or fanciful shapes by regular pruning and clipping of the twigs – has been practised since Roman times. Evergreen species that are resilient to regular clipping are the most popular victims, with Box proving the most malleable and popular of all. A well-managed, rectangular garden hedge is a simple and utilitarian form of topiary.

Buxaceae, the family that includes our Box, belongs to a group of ancient flowering plant families that, in evolutionary terms, preceded nearly all the others. It is a

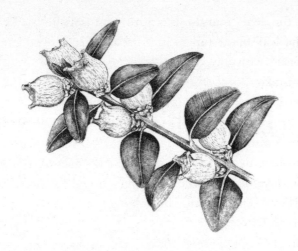

cosmopolitan family, but the 94 species of *Buxus*, the largest genus, are centred on the tropics or subtropics. Of these, only our Box is frost tolerant. It grows in Western Europe and North Africa and borders the Mediterranean as far as the Caucasus. It was one of the key players of the laurisilva forest that dominated a much warmer, wetter Britain before the Ice Age. When Box returned to Britain after the ice retreated, it did not do so with great enthusiasm and remained in the south, seeking out the south-facing chalk slopes that warm up quickly in the spring. Nowadays in Britain, it is grown widely in much of England as a manicured ornamental and suburban hedging plant, but it cannot survive in the far north. In fact, it is found very rarely growing naturally in the wild, only in two locations: Box Hill, Surrey, and Boxley, Kent.

Like most tropical rainforest species, Box has glossy evergreen leaves, but these are very small, only 2 cm long. The leaves are poisonous and arranged in opposite pairs, and the leaf margin is entire (not serrated). The base of the leaf blade tapers into its stem. It is not likely to be confused with any of our other native species, but it may be mistaken for *Lonicera nitida* (Box Honeysuckle), also used in garden hedges. The latter has even smaller leaves, which have truncate or heart-shaped bases to the leaf blade. One of the poisonous active ingredients in Box is cyclobuxine, a steroidal alkaloid that occurs in the leaves and bark. This strong alkaloid has recently been studied for the treatment of HIV/AIDS and may have potential for Alzheimer's and other diseases.

Box flowers are tiny (1mm), without petals, and unisexual – though one female flower, surrounded by five or six male flowers (with four stamens each) occur in the same tiny cluster, making Box monoecious. The flowers open very early in the year and are easily missed. They produce nectar, so are equipped to be insect-pollinated, and Box nectar is eagerly foraged during this season, when there is not much else about. Hoverflies, Houseflies and Honey Bees are attracted visually by the clusters of bright yellow anthers. After pollination, the female flower in the centre develops into a green, six-seeded capsule.

Box

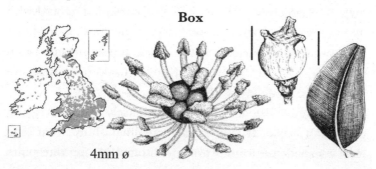

4mm ø

Box wood is fine-grained and the hardest native wood in Europe. It doesn't have knots or growth rings and, as a result, has been a favourite wood for sculptors and engravers across the centuries. It was used for woodblock printing and for chess pieces, unstained for the white and stained for the black, in lieu of ebony. In the music industry, it is used for making tailpieces, chin rests and tuning pegs for stringed instruments.

This tree's occurrence on Box Hill was recognised early on to be of commercial potential. It is highly likely that the presence of Box trees here was supplemented artificially by planting as a means of conserving, perpetuating and extending the population in order to sustain the industry. Cheaper timber from Portugal led to the collapse of the Box wood trade in 1797, by which time the Box groves on this famous hill were well established.

CELASTRACEAE

Spindle *Euonymus europaeus*

Those who live in Spindle country will almost certainly agree that this hedgerow plant is the most eagerly anticipated for its autumn colouration. The leaves turn glorious tones of pink, orange and purple and the shocking pink capsules, with their seeds completely coated in a bright-orange aril, seem unnaturally exotic in the British landscape.

Spindle belongs to the predominantly tropical family, the Celastraceae. It is the only member of the family to have escaped the tropics and penetrated so far north into

temperate regions. This might explain the flamboyance of its colourful fruit.

Spindle is most common in the south of Britain, where it is typically found in hedgerows and is sometimes associated with Dogwood as scrub on chalk or limestone downland. It is unusual to find it growing in isolation. It is less common further north and cannot survive in the far north of Britain. In some southern counties it is considered to be an ancient woodland indicator species, but although it is shade-tolerant, it is more often found growing along woodland margins.

The seeds are toxic, but the arils are nourishing – more so than the fruits of any other native tree or shrub. Robins are the chief consumers, followed by Blackcaps and tits. All discard the seed nearby.

The leaves are simple, opposite, very finely serrated (use a lens), and twice as long as wide. The twigs are unusual in that

155

Spindle

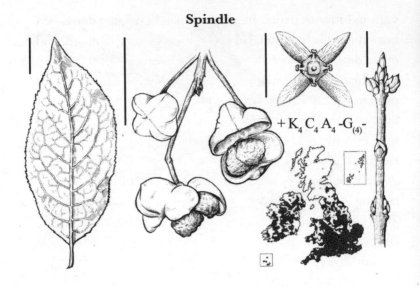

$$+ K_4 C_4 A_4 \text{-} G_{(4)}\text{-}$$

they remain green for at least three years. This characteristic is a particularly useful ID feature, as the twigs of most of our other trees turn brown well within the first year. From the second year on, many twigs often develop corky ridges – also a characteristic of Field Maple and English Elm.

Spindle flowers in early summer, in stalked clusters of up to 10. The small flowers are greenish-cream in colour. Nectar is secreted by a distinct nectar disc at the base of the four stamens. Flies are the chief pollinators.

The four-lobed pink capsule splits open to reveal four to six seeds, each coated in a bright orange aril. Only nature (and my best friend, and artist, Jenny) could combine these two colours and get away with it.

Despite the nutritional value of the aril, the seeds are poisonous to birds and mammals, including humans. They contain, among other substances, a cardiac glycoside and various bitter terpenes. Ingestion can at best cause diarrhoea but more likely results in liver and kidney damage and even death. Powdered Spindle fruits were once used to treat head lice and mange. Strong anti-herbivore chemicals present in the leaves fail to deter a good range of insect larvae, including the Spindle Ermine Moth and many aphid species, which in turn provide food for a range of predatory ladybirds and earwigs.

Spindle wood is very hard and was used in the past for making butchers' skewers and spindles for wool spinning. Today, Spindle is used to make top-quality charcoal for artists. Cultivated forms of the tree are grown in gardens for their autumn colour.

SALICACEAE – AN INTRODUCTION

Members of this family were among the first trees to spread back into the tundra landscape of Britain at the end of the Ice Age. Indeed, the many prostrate willow species (outside the scope of this book) were already an integral part of the sparse tundra community that first colonised the wide, open, rock-strewn plateaux. All Salicaceae are symbiotic with ectomycorrhizal fungi, which gave the pioneers a huge advantage in this seriously inhospitable terrain.

Black Poplar (but not Aspen) and all the willows (except Goat) are typically associated with wet habitats. These are the shrubs and trees that colonise the edges of swamps, bogs, fens and marshes. Wetland habitats are relatively inaccessible to humans, making them one of our least disturbed havens for wildlife; the often impenetrable thicket of willows (known as willow 'carr') that surrounds them plays an important role in providing cover and nesting sites for many animals. Sadly, over the last thousand years, most of our wetlands have been drained to make way for rich grazing land or agriculture. The broad, flat, lowland floodplains of our many rivers no longer teem with wildlife. Similarly, many species of butterflies and dragonflies associated with our upland bogs have become increasingly scarce due to loss of wetland habitat.

Now we are left with a ribbon of mostly Salicaceae trees and shrubs flanking the rivers. The tall, graceful Crack and White Willows (and if you're lucky, Black Poplar) are a gorgeous part of the scene with sometimes dense, mixed thickets of Osier, Grey, Purple, Bay or Almond Willows. Some line wet drainage ditches alongside roads, often forming the main constituent of roadside hedge banks. All plants require water, but unlike willows, few can tolerate airless, waterlogged soils. The same goes for the mycorrhizal fungi. So, despite being a mycorrhizal community, willow carr does not have a rich variety of toadstools.

The flowers of poplars and willows are without petals and borne in unisexual catkins, with male and female catkins occurring on separate trees – they are dioecious, like Yew, Juniper and Holly. This guarantees cross-pollination and eliminates the negative genetic consequences of inbreeding, via self-pollination.

Poplar Catkin ♂

Willow Catkin ♂

The catkins of poplars are different from those of willows in two fundamental ways. First, and most obvious, poplar catkins dangle, while willow catkins are more rigid and often upright.

Second, alongside each of the willow florets that make up a catkin, there is a tiny nectary that is absent from poplar florets. (These are tricky to see even with a hand lens – but worth the challenge.)

These clues alert you to the fact that poplars are wind-pollinated – their male catkins shake their pollen into the wind. However, unlike poplars and most catkin-bearing trees, willows are typically insect-pollinated. Their catkins are firm enough to allow bees to clamber over them, collecting pollen whilst on the hunt for the nectar found in tiny rations in those miniscule nectaries.

Once fertilised, the female organs of the female catkins of both genera turn into seed-packed capsules. When these are mature, they split open to release hundreds of tiny plumed seeds that are dispersed by the wind.

Osier – Fruiting Catkin

7mm long closed capsule with nectary

On warm, sunny afternoons in late May, the air can be filled with millions of floating plumed seeds that will drift in air currents for long distances. Such wind dispersal of countless propagules is characteristic of opportunistic species – those that seize the opportunity of colonising a freshly exposed habitat. In the case of the Salicaceae, this means wet habitats, or at least wet soils. Thus begins the process of succession through to mature woodland. The willows 'suck' water from the ground, and if this is not replenished, other species will find the now drier soil more acceptable. Eventually, the willows and poplars will be squeezed out of the wood by the shade of taller tree species but, many decades on, they may still be hanging on around the woodland margins, ready to invade any clearings. High numbers of willows or Aspens forming the main body of a wood indicate that it is still a young, or 'secondary', wood.

This opportunistic propensity to invade open habitats accounts for the predominance of Grey Willow and Aspen amongst the pioneering trees that first spread into the open ground of the British Isles 11,000 years ago once the ice had retreated and where the ground had begun to thaw.

SALICACEAE

Aspen *Populus tremula*
Black Poplar *Populus nigra*

Black Poplar
fruiting catkin

When a breeze disturbs the leaves of an Aspen tree, the effect is extraordinary. Close your eyes and you immediately picture a babbling brook; open them and the flickering of light off the fluttering leaves confirms the impression – sunlight dancing on the surface of the rippling water. The sound and vision of Aspens and other poplars can be wonderfully soothing and restorative. Another mystical and reassuring 'poplar' scene is the gradual emergence of a majestic Black Poplar through the early morning autumn mists – a calm sentinel on a lowland riverbank.

These are our two native poplars. We have made the arbitrary decision to ignore the well-established and beautiful introduction from Europe – White Poplar, *Populus alba* – and a native-born hybrid between Aspen and White Poplar: Grey Poplar, *Populus x canescens*. There are also many Black Poplar hybrids which share the same magical beauty of all poplars.

Aspen was one of the early pioneers after the ice retreated. It didn't need to wait for the ground to thaw. In Britain today, it is one of the first trees to colonise bare ground. It does not require its feet to be wet, like most willows and other poplars. Not only does Aspen spread effectively via its wind-dispersed seeds, but it can also quickly take over a large area by sending up numerous young shoots (suckers) from its widely spreading shallow roots. The suckers grow quickly into trees but still maintain underground connection with all the others arising from the original specimen. They are all effectively part of the same plant. Think about this when you next come across a spinney of Aspens. In Utah there is a closely related tree – the Quaking Aspen, *Populus tremuloides* – where one plant has sent up 47,000 trunks covering an area of 108 acres (44 hectares). It is thought to weigh 6 million kilograms – probably the largest single tree in the world. There must be similar unstudied examples of *Populus tremula* in the boreal forests of northern Europe.

Although this is remarkable, it is potentially catastrophic. If disease hits, it will not only spread rapidly from tree to tree via their connected roots, but every 'individual' is genetically the same. There will be no genetic variability that might offer resistance to the pathogen. And because, like willows, all poplars are dioecious, the whole forest is the same sex, which means that no seed can be produced (unless there is another clone of the opposite sex within pollination distance).

Historically, Black Poplar was almost certainly restricted to the wide, lowland floodplains of southern Britain, where there were once extensive woodlands probably dominated by this fabulous tree. The drainage of those floodplains and felling for timber dramatically reduced the Black Poplar's distribution to scattered individuals along the riverbanks, where it has an uncertain future. The dwindling population of the dioecious Black Poplar has resulted in wide separation of the sexes. Consequently, the opportunities for spread by sexual reproduction and seed are extremely limited. It does not sucker readily like Aspen, but country folk have long valued Black Poplar wood and so have propagated it by vegetative means. This has resulted in genetically identical, single-sex clones of trees forming local populations with the same potential dangers as associated with the genetically uniform Aspen woods described above.

Aspen is currently widespread and secure. But the map for Black Poplar disguises the threat to its future. (One dot in a 10km by 10km square may refer only to one individual tree.)

Aspen

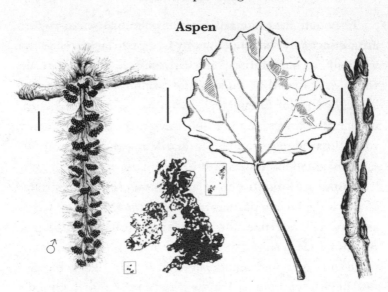

♂

Black Poplar

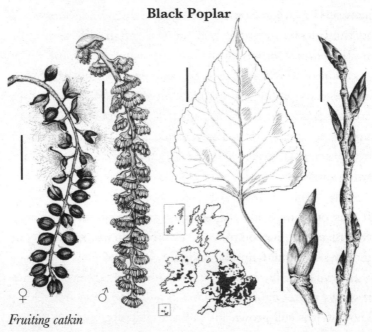

♀   ♂

Fruiting catkin

They both have alternately arranged simple leaves, which are distinctively shaped. Aspen leaves flutter in the slightest wind in a characteristic way attributable to the petiole, which is flattened at right angles to the plane of the leaf blade. Beware of Grey Poplar leaves – which look like large, hairy Aspen leaves – and the various hybrids of Black Poplar, whose leaves are variations on the same theme.

Poplar catkins burst early in the year long before the leaves and are fantastic, especially close up. The male catkins of Black Poplar are particularly striking, with their wine-red anthers. After fertilisation each female catkin becomes a spray of neat, round capsules that turn 'woolly' and untidy when they burst and relinquish their plumed seeds.

The winter buds of all poplars tend to be appressed against the twigs. Some appear to stick out sideways, but turn out to be terminal buds at the tips of very short side stalks. Unlike willows, their buds have more than three bud scales, which are hairless. Aspen twigs are dark, shiny and slightly sticky, while Black Poplar's (and its hybrids) are matt, despite being sticky, and are yellow-brown. The tips of its appressed lateral buds often curve outwards in a characteristic way. (White and Grey Poplars have hairy twigs and buds.)

The wood of Black Poplar is springy and fire-resistant. It was once used for cart wheels and wagon bottoms, and extensively for floorboards and thatching spars – especially in the days of candles and oil lamps.

Grey Poplar has been a valued forestry tree. Being a hybrid, it grows more vigorously than other *Populus* species. I don't know if it is still grown for the manufacture of matchsticks, but in Suffolk in the 1970s, I used to walk students through a Grey Poplar plantation that was owned by Bryant and May.

SALICACEAE

Bay Willow *Salix pentandra*
Crack Willow *Salix x fragilis*
White Willow *Salix alba*
Almond Willow *Salix triandra*
Purple Willow *Salix purpurea*
Osier *Salix viminalis*
Goat Willow *Salix caprea*
Grey Willow *Salix cinerea*

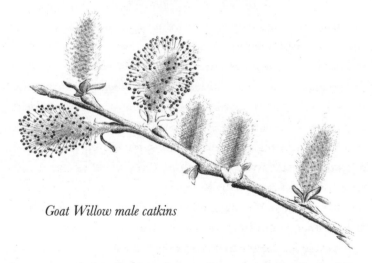

Goat Willow male catkins

One summer in the noughties, when we were in the West Country, Nell helped me with a wetland plant survey that involved kayaking through dense reed beds and sedge swamps, and across open water to reach some floating islands that had been colonised by dense thickets of Grey Willow – a fascinating and enriching experience. It's not every day that one has the privilege to explore such a pristine and exquisite piece of flower-rich woodland that rocks like a boat when its canopy catches the wind.

Willows have the reputation of being impossible to identify, but we hope to dispel that defeatist view. In Britain there are 20 different species of willows and it is said that 'they all look alike' – they don't. But they all hybridise freely with each other and, what's more, willow hybrids are sexually fertile, unlike many hybrids (think of the mule – an infertile hybrid between a horse and a donkey). They are able to cross with other willow species, resulting in a bewildering collection of over 70 hybrid mixtures.

This can complicate matters when identifying a particular tree. However, the hybrids are not as widespread as the parents and often a hybrid can be deduced because, unsurprisingly, it has a combination of traits from both parents.

More confusing for the beginner is the degree of variation within each species, giving rise to a number of accepted varieties which might be taken for hybrids. But don't let these complications stop you having a go. More often than not, you will correctly recognise the most likely candidate(s) – a big step forward from simply saying 'willow'. But if you sometimes draw a blank – join the band of many before you!

So for now, forget hybrids. The first step is to recognise the species. And this isn't really a *very* difficult task, especially when you see that we can whittle it down from the possible 20 to only 8 species. We will not be considering the six tundra species that grow as prostrate mats in the Arctic and at the tops of our Scottish mountains. We are also excluding the four low shrubby species that did not meet our arbitrary selection criterion of reaching over 4 metres in height. Finally, we exclude the two scarce, recent alien species that you are unlikely to come across in the wild. This leaves us with the eight commonly occurring species that can stand over 5 metres tall. Once you become familiar with these eight, you will be able to spot hybrids, and you might want to explore the low-growing shrubs of bogs and sand dunes or discover the amazing dwarf montane pioneers. The hunt for willows can lead you to some truly special habitats.

All but one willow have spirally (alternately) arranged leaves and hence buds. Purple Willow (see below) is the exception. The buds of willows (unlike those of poplars) are unique in being wrapped in only one bud scale. This is an extremely useful ID characteristic to grasp. The buds of most willows are slender and flattened against the stem – appressed. The prominent buds of Goat Willow are the exception.

In winter, it is difficult, but not impossible, to distinguish between all the willows by their twigs and buds. Colour and hairiness are useful features but can vary considerably between different plants of the same species and they also change throughout the winter months – for example, starting hairy and yellow, becoming bald and brown. Leaf features are more straightforward, so use characteristics of the leaves as far as possible – even dead leaves beneath the tree can provide some clues.

All willow leaves are simple and several share similar shapes. Not all are long and narrow and adorning pendulous branches

Willow Twigs

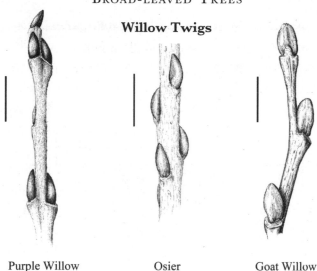

Purple Willow   Osier   Goat Willow

– which is most people's expectation, based on the cultivated Weeping Willows of parks and gardens. Six of our eight species fall into two groups according to their leaf shape. Osier, Crack and White Willow have long, narrow leaves – over five times as long as wide. Goat, Grey and Bay Willow are broad – less than three times as long as wide. Because of their natural variability, Almond and Purple Willows do not always fit neatly into one group, but have other distinguishing features.

From Nell's illustrations of typical specimens, it is possible to distinguish them all from each other on the basis of shape and dimensions. But in reality you seldom have the other leaves at hand with which to compare and contrast. The leaves of a single tree can also vary widely in size (and, less so, in shape). So consider other features in conjunction with shape, such as the leaf margins and hairiness. Where you can, select leaves from mature branches, as these tend to be more 'typical'.

Narrow-leaved Willows Key – Based Primarily on Leaves

Narrow-leaved	Osier	Crack Willow	White Willow	Almond Willow
Leaf Dimensions length/width	15 x 1.5cm (10x)	13 x 2cm (6x)	11 x 1.5cm (7x)	8 x 2cm (4x)
Leaf Margin	Entire & undercurled	Coarsely serrated	Finely serrated	Finely serrated
Hairs	Hairy	Hairless	Hairy	Hairless
Upper Surface	Dull green & slightly hairy	Bright green & shiny	Dark green & dull with scattered hairs	Dark green & dull
Lower Surface	Silky appressed hairs	Waxy, blue/green	Silky, appressed hairs	Paler or waxy
Twigs & Buds (all appressed)	Hairy, buds blunt; twigs become hairless	Hairless; buds olive brown; twigs snap easily at base	Hairy; buds reddish-brown	Hairless; buds blunt often reddish

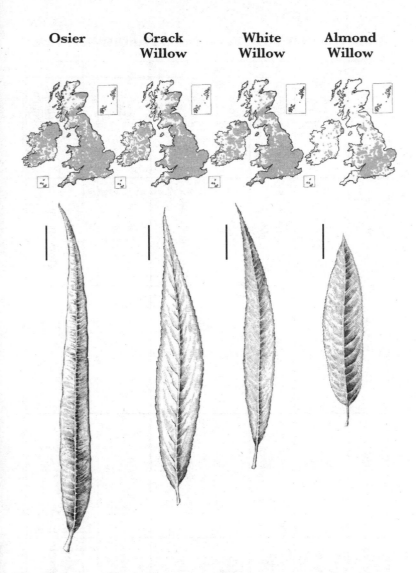

Osier **Crack Willow** **White Willow** **Almond Willow**

Broad-leaved Willows Key – Based Primarily on Leaves

Broad-leaved	Purple Willow	Grey Willow	Goat Willow	Bay Willow
Leaf Dimensions length/width	6 x 1.7cm (3.5x)	7 x 3cm (2x)	8 x 6cm (1.5x)	9 x 3cm (3x)
Leaf Margin	Entire at base; serrated towards tip	Crenate to entire	Crenate-serrate to entire	Uniformly serrate, with lumpy glands
Hairs	Hairless	Hairy	Hairy	Hairless
Leaf Surfaces	Dark above, paler below	Dark, dull upper; grey, hairy lower with rusty hairs on veins	Grey hairy lower	Shiny on both, Paler green lower
Key Features	Leaves opposite or sub-opposite	Obovate shape (i.e. broader towards the tip)	Twisted tip to leaf	Small glands on petiole – scent of bay
Twig & Buds	Buds opposite, reddish	Hairy; appressed, reddish buds	Hairless; prominent, yellow (to brown) buds	Hairless; dark, glossy, slightly prominent buds

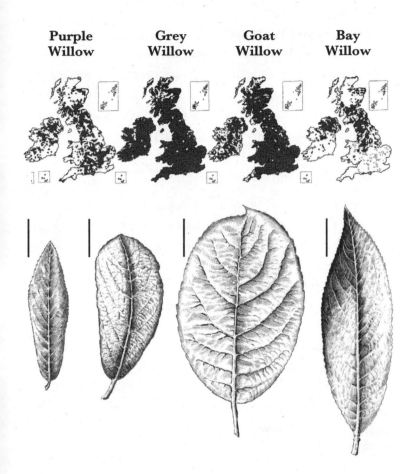

173

Narrow-leaved Willows
(Osier, Crack, White and Almond)

Osier, Crack, White and Almond Willow are strictly non-native, but were introduced by early man (so they are archaeophytes). They are so well established that most people view them as native, so we have included them as honorary natives.

Almond Willow and Osier

The young twigs and branches of Almond Willow and Osier are particularly flexible and were highly valued for wicker work at a time when wicker was the norm for furniture, fish traps, baskets, prams, coffins and many other items. Nowadays, wickerwork has become fashionable again. Almond Willow and Osier and their hybrids are extremely fast-growing and productive during the first two years after coppicing and are cultivated and harvested in withy beds to supply not only the wicker market, but also the biomass industry.

Osier is easily distinguished from the other long, thin-leaved species by its entire, slightly under-curled margin. The unique feature of mature Almond Willows is the grey bark that peels off in broad flakes.

Crack and White Willow

Crack and White Willows are often confused with each other, particularly since they both exist in a variety of distinct forms and the hybrids between them are well established. But focused observation helps to distinguish them. Crack Willow leaves are hairless, a shiny green above and a waxy blue-green (glaucous) below. White Willow leaves are a darker, duller green above and the lower surface has a coating of fine silver hairs lying flat (appressed) against it (use a lens). Sometimes their branches 'weep'. But the true Weeping Willows are cultivated hybrids between Crack or White Willow and the original weeping species that was introduced from China via the Silk Road in 1730. The Chinese introduction has since become extinct in Britain.

The twigs of Crack Willow break off cleanly with a snap, and when the branches break off, they do so cleanly with a loud crack. Like all willows, young twigs root easily in damp soil, so when twigs and branches fall from trees overhanging rivers, they wash downstream until they get lodged in a bank, where they grow into new trees. This attribute is exploited in environmental projects to create withy beds for recycling and filtering water naturally, as well as to provide a habitat for a whole host of riverside wildlife.

White Willow has two claims to fame. The wood obtained from one of its varieties is notably shock- and splinter-resistant and is used for making cricket bats. The other is salicin, present in the bark and leaves of all willows (and some other plants), but first discovered and most abundant in White Willow. Salicin breaks down into salicylic acid when a leaf is damaged in any way. This chemical is a hormone that plays a number of important roles in the plant, one being to trigger the production of toxic or unpalatable defence chemicals in response to the damage caused by a pathogenic infection. This is analogous to the innate immune system found in animals. It has also been discovered that volatile esters of salicylic acid are simultaneously emitted by the infected plant. These diffuse through the atmosphere and are quickly detected and responded to by other plants.

Willow bark, its active ingredient salicin and its derivative, salicylic acid – have long been recognised as compounds that relieve pain and reduce fever. Salicin's medicinal importance to mankind has been documented since 5000 BP. Nowadays, a synthetic derivative of salicylic acid – acetylated salicylic acid – has been chemically manufactured and marketed under the trade name 'aspirin'. When we first moved to Kent, our immediate neighbour was a beautiful grey horse called Paris. Sadly, she suffered from arthritis. She knew about the link between willows and pain relief. On bad days she'd invariably be seen gnawing at the bark of the Crack Willow in her field. I hope it helped her – it didn't do the willow much good.

Broad-leaved Willows (Bay, Goat, Grey and Purple)

Unlike the narrow-leaved species, the four broad-leaved species are all native to Britain.

Purple and Bay Willow

Purple Willow leaves are arranged in (almost) opposite pairs, unlike the rest. Its purple-twigged hybrids with Osier and Almond Willow are popular in basketry.

Bay Willow leaves are hairless and shiny on both surfaces. This species is found in northern Europe, and it occurs naturally in northern England – but, strangely, not far north into Scotland. Most occurrences south of the Wash and the Severn are likely to be male specimens and of garden origin, since male plants are considered to be particularly attractive. Crush a leaf – aromatic glands, visible near the top of the petiole, emit a faint, spicy aroma supposedly reminiscent of culinary Bay, which, sadly, I have never been able to detect.

Goat and Grey Willow

Goat is the willow that has a wide distribution, often occurring some distance from water, and Grey occurs more widely in Britain than any other native tree species.

The leaves of Goat Willow are egg-shaped with, almost invariably, twisted tips, while Grey Willow leaves are broader towards the tip, obovate, i.e. an upside-down egg shape.

The Goat Willow is often known as the Great Sallow and Grey as Common Sallow. Both share the name Pussy Willow. The lovely catkins of most willows, but particularly these two, start soft and silky like kittens' mittens (hence 'Pussy') before they open out into their fabulous 'bottlebrush' design. Except for Bay Willow, our native species and Osier develop catkins before their leaves occasionally in February, but normally in March or April. Bay Willow and all the archaeophytes, except Osier, produce their catkins at the same time as the leaves, usually in April, May or sometimes June.

Second only to the oaks, willow leaves provide an important food supply for a wide variety and number of insects and other invertebrates. For example, Grey Willow leaves are the main food plant of the caterpillars of the Purple Emperor butterfly, a magnificent but elusive species whose numbers have declined dramatically, as more and more wetland is drained to make way for agriculture.

Goat willow is the earliest to come into flower, and does so long before its leaves burst. Its nectar provides a vital source of energy for insects early in the year when there is not much food about. On a warm, sunny day in February or March, you can sometimes hear a grove of willows before you see it – the hum of thousands of happy bees.

Such a wealth of insect life early in the season is likely to attract insect-eating birds, such as tits. And some, notably Blue Tits, will also be foraging for the energy-rich nectar. The feeding activity of these birds can result in viable pollination – so bird pollination is not the prerogative of hummingbirds and sunbirds in the tropics.

ROSACEAE – AN INTRODUCTION

Most of our trees that produce abundant blossom belong to the rose family. They are amongst some of our most spectacular when in flower and again in autumn colour. They include our orchard trees – apples, pears, plums and cherries, and also quinces, medlars and peaches. Native members of the family include Hawthorn, Wild Cherry, Crab Apple, Rowan and Whitebeam.

None of them becomes dominant in any woodland ecosystem. None of them forms EcM partnerships, so they are not supported directly by the extensive and highly efficient Wood Wide Web of EcM. However, they are all supported by arbuscular mycorrhizal networks. A few, such as Midland Hawthorn, Wild Service and Wild Cherry, are shade-tolerant, but the rest cling to clearings or woodland margins – or prefer to join an open scrub community. We find them peppering the woodlands and hedgerows or out in the open country, like Rowan and Hawthorn. With their seasonal beauty, they act as a harbinger of spring and as bearers of autumn bounty.

The basic floral design, common to all members of the family, is unique among our trees. The giveaway feature is the mass of stamens – more than twice the number of petals.

Cherry Flower

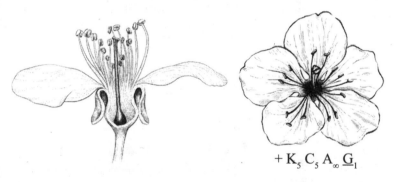

$$+ K_5 \, C_5 \, A_\infty \, \underline{G}_1$$

The gynoecium sits in a cup called the hypanthium. The number of carpels making up the gynoecium is one, two, three or five (count the styles). They always remain separate/free from each other, though often embedded close together in the hypanthium, which usually develops into a fleshy false fruit.

The fruits of all the species are edible and nutritious, to attract mammals and birds for dispersing their seeds. But their seeds contain amygdalin, a cyanogenic glycoside, which releases hydrogen cyanide if the seed coat is damaged. The seeds are bitter to the taste and are therefore rejected during

Haw

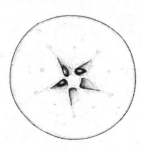

Apple

Cherry

ingestion or swallowed whole and later regurgitated or excreted elsewhere unharmed. The leaf and bud arrangement is always alternate, but the leaves may be simple, lobed or compound.

The top of a false fruit, such as an apple or a haw, will bear the remains of the flower, particularly five shrivelled sepals, because the fleshy part is derived from the hypanthium. The ovary wall of the Hawthorns turns into a woody nut, while the five (or three) ovary walls of apple, Whitebeam, etc. remain thin and become the five (or three) chambers of the core in the centre of the succulent and nourishing hypanthium. There are no flower remains at the tip of the drupe – only a tiny scar left by the discarded style. This is because the fleshy part and the stone are derived from the ovary wall. It is a true fruit. The rest of the flower, including the hypanthium, withers away. Here are our nine species arranged according to their leaf shape and fruit type.

Rosaceae Species by Leaf and Fruit

		Drupe	Haw (nuts buried in hypanthium)	Pomme (core buried in hypanthium)
Simple		**Blackthorn** **Wild Cherry** **Bird Cherry**		**Crab Apple** **Whitebeam**
Lobed			**Hawthorn** **Midland Hawthorn**	**Wild Service**
Compound				**Rowan**

ROSACEAE

Blackthorn *Prunus spinosa*
Wild Cherry *Prunus avium*
Bird Cherry *Prunus padus*

Blackthorn flowers smother the spiny, leafless branches of the dark hedgerows sometimes as early as late February. It is one of the earliest trees to provide nectar and pollen and to signal that spring is on its way. It is the most ubiquitous of all our *Prunus* species, thinning out further north in Scotland, and is absent from the Highlands and the outer isles. It migrated back into Britain about 8000 BP but, being light-demanding, it expanded its range only after Neolithic farmers opened up the forest.

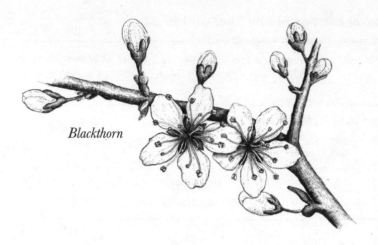

Blackthorn

Wild Cherry returned more recently, around 7000 BP, just early enough to get across to Ireland before it became an island. It is more tolerant of shade than Blackthorn, so is able to coexist comfortably in mature woodland. Today, it has a similarly wide distribution to Blackthorn, though it is less abundant, particularly in the north and west. It produces masses of umbels of about two to six larger, longer-stalked flowers just before the leaves. On a breezy day the petals drop like confetti.

Bird Cherry produces glorious chains (racemes) of flowers along with its leaves and is found naturally inside or outside woodlands, but only in more northern regions and on more basic soils. Unsurprisingly, it was the first of the three to return to Britain in about 10,000 BP. However, due to its inability to form ectomycorrhizal associations, it could not be a pioneer, but once the pioneer trees had paved the way, Bird Cherry was amongst the next batch of trees to grace our islands.

The leaves of our three *Prunus* species are similar in shape – twice as long as wide, and with an evenly serrated margin. Those of Blackthorn are markedly smaller compared with the cherries. The petioles of both cherrys' leaves are equipped with a pair of extrafloral nectaries – two glistening red lumps close to the leaf blade. These nectary glands are designed to attract a host of invertebrates for a purpose other than pollination. The bright red colour and the associated nectar attract predatory insects, such as ants and parasitic wasps, which will feed not only on the 'nectar' but also any leaf-eating insects nearby, thus protecting the tree. In autumn, cherry leaves usually turn spectacular shades of red and orange.

The bark of mature cherry trees is easily spotted because it develops characteristic horizontal splits. In winter the bud scales of the two cherries are a different colour. Wild Cherry has rich brown buds, while those of Bird Cherry are dark, almost black, with pale edges. An excellent ID feature of Wild Cherry, but not Bird Cherry, is the stubby lateral branchlets set back from the tip of the leading shoots. They terminate in a cluster of buds – easy to spot from the ground below. The tiny Blackthorn buds are closely arranged along the short, spine-tipped side twigs. Branches and twigs of the cherries are unarmed. Both Blackthorn and Wild Cherry spread enthusiastically via root suckers, giving rise to dense thickets. The spiny Blackthorn thickets are particularly impenetrable and make ideal cover for nesting birds.

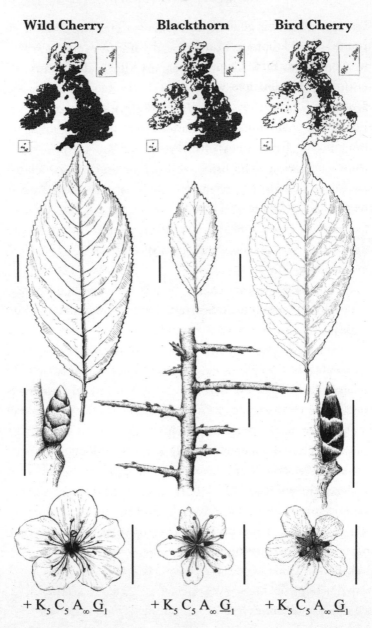

Wild Cherry **Blackthorn** **Bird Cherry**

$+ K_5 C_5 A_\infty \underline{G}_1$ $+ K_5 C_5 A_\infty \underline{G}_1$ $+ K_5 C_5 A_\infty \underline{G}_1$

The species of this genus flower in different months – Blackthorn in March, Wild Cherry in April and Bird Cherry in May. This ensures that pollinators focus on one species at a time. This greatly favours legitimate and successful pollination. All *Prunus* species develop true fruits known as drupes. Each drupe contains a single seed within a stony case surrounded by succulent flesh. The rest of the flower, including the hypanthium, withers away. Blackthorn drupes are more commonly known as sloes. They are like small, round plums, about 1cm long, and blue-black, with a waxy bloom. Wild Cherry drupes hang usually in pairs and are dark red, while those of Bird Cherry are small, black and arranged in a raceme. Fresh sloes off the bush are unpalatably bitter. Even so, they were eaten by late Neolithic people, along with both the cherries. Personally, we think sloes are much more palatable steeped for several months in gin with sugar, and the flavoured gin is not bad either!

Cultivated sweet cherries come in many varieties, all derived from our Wild Cherry. While Sweet Cherries are tasty and contain vitamin C, they do not contain many other health-promoting ingredients that are found in the skin and flesh of the fruits of the bitter Bird Cherry and Blackthorn. These two species, despite lacking appeal, are rich in beneficial phenolic

Winter twig
of Wild
Cherry

compounds and anthocyanins, which are antioxidants that help prevent cardiovascular diseases, cancer, diabetes and age-related conditions.

Meanwhile, as with most Rosaceae, the seed coat releases hydrogen cyanide when damaged. But the stone of the drupe of *Prunus* species protects the seed from damage, and hence the consumer and disperser from poison. The cyanogenic glycosides are also concentrated in the bark of Bird Cherry. Until the advent of industrial agricultural pesticides in the 1950s, Bird Cherry bark was spread on potato fields and apple orchards by some farmers in the north of the country to deter rodent and insect pests.

ROSACEAE

Crab Apple *Malus sylvestris*

There are few scenes that bring back such nostalgic memories as the golden carpet that surrounds the trunk of a Crab Apple tree in the autumn. Or so say Sue and Jen, Nell's cousins, who fondly remember childhood days collecting basket-loads of fruit for their mother to make exquisite crab-apple jelly.

People have enjoyed Crab Apple since its late arrival to our shores, sneaking in just in time to get across to Ireland.

It is light-demanding and favours good, moist soils. Despite its scientific name – *M. sylvestris*, meaning 'of the woods' – it prefers the more open habitats of hedgerow and scrub, and only became significant in the pollen record during the Bronze Age, when forest clearance was a more common feature of the landscape.

It is a small tree, typically, but not invariably, equipped with blunt thorns. The fruit are not normally eaten off the tree, being very sour. This is attributable to particularly high concentrations of malic acid, which is present in all plants for the vital role it plays in photosynthesis. Malic acid also tends to accumulate in fruits and was first identified in apples – hence its name. It occurs in notably high concentrations in all Rosaceae fruits, is the prominent taste of rhubarb, and occurs in grapes, lending tartness to wine. Crab Apples are also rich in pectin, a natural gelling agent. In the plant, this helps bind cell walls together. The softening of fruit is associated with the breakdown of pectin as the fruit ripens. In the kitchen, the Crab Apple's pectin facilitates the transformation of its juice into a delicately spicy, ruby-coloured jelly.

Cultivated apples often occur in the wild, having grown from discarded apple cores. But Crab Apple is distinct. It has small, yellow, hard and very sour fruit, and leaves that are hairless underneath. Orchard apple leaves are hairy. All apples have five (or four) separate carpels. The styles fuse briefly into one before they emerge from the centre of the flower and then separate again, into five stigmas. After fertilisation of the ovules (one or two in each ovary), the five ovary walls become the star-shaped core. The flesh of the apple is a false fruit derived from the swollen hypanthium, with the remains of the flower on the top. Look closely at the illustration below (or at a real apple). There are 10 dots. These are the traces of 10 veins that passed up the flower stalk and hypanthium to feed the 5 sepals and 5 petals.

Crab Apple

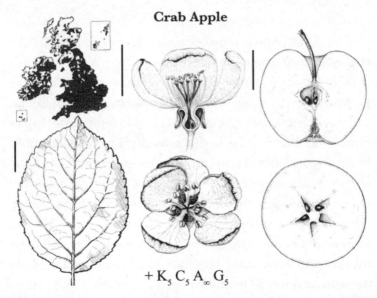

$$+ K_5 \, C_5 \, A_\infty \, G_5$$

Wild Pears are very similar in flower and fruit but they are doubtfully native and uncommon, so we are not covering them here.

Crab Apple is one of over 40 wild apples found globally, almost all in northern temperate regions. They are collectively referred to as 'crab apples' to distinguish them from those that are cultivated as a crop. The ancestor of the cultivated orchard apple, *Malus domestica* and its many varieties, is believed to be the crab apple from the mountains of southern Kazakhstan, *Malus sieversii*, but other crabs, including ours (strictly called the European Crab), also contributed some genes by cross-breeding to create the many varieties.

Our Crab Apple is self-fertile, so a lone Crab Apple can produce fruit with viable seed. Most of the cultivated varieties are so self-sterile that single-variety orchards usually require individual trees of another variety or species to provide pollen in order to ensure that fruit is set. Our Crab Apple was traditionally employed in this pollinator role since it has a long flowering season, enabling one Crab Apple tree to serve different orchard apple varieties, flowering at staggered times. It was encouraged in the surrounding hedgerows or planted within the orchard. Now, exotic crabs are more often used because they attract fewer potential pests.

ROSACEAE

Hawthorn *Crataegus monogyna*
Midland Hawthorn *Crataegus laevigata*

Midland Hawthorn is a shade-tolerant southerner that avoids chalk. It seldom grows naturally outside the forest environment and, as such, it is a good indicator of ancient woodland. It flowers and comes into leaf early in the year before the main canopy develops.

Hawthorn is more light-demanding and although often found on the edges of woodland, it flourishes better in hedgerows and scattered about in open country on a range of soils, from coastal shingle to chalk downs to heathland and open moorland. Although it is now the more common of the two, before forest clearance began (5000 BP) it must have been a scarce outsider, found teetering on unstable, dry river banks or clinging to cliff faces – places where woodland was unable to establish.

So in the past, these two species seldom grew naturally alongside each other, even where their distribution overlapped. But now that our woodlands are fragmented, they often occur together along a wood margin or in a hedgerow, and cross-pollination is common. There are no natural barriers to cross-fertilisation and the hybrid thorn *Crataegus x media* is the result.

Our two thorns are superficially very similar, but easily distinguished. The winter twigs are characteristic. The buds are tiny and the scales are hard to see, even with a lens. However, their alternately arranged leaves are markedly different – deeply and sharply lobed in Hawthorn, but only three shallow and rounded lobes in Midland Hawthorn. The haws contain one nutlet in Hawthorn but two in Midland Hawthorn. This is reflected in the number of styles emerging from the top of the haw or the centre of the flower. Check several haws or flowers on the plant you are examining.

In the Midlands, East Anglia and the southeast, many trees don't match either species neatly, but lie somewhere between the two. These will most likely be the hybrid thorn.

Hawthorn was eager to return to Britain as the ice retreated, but played only a minor role until Neolithic farmers started clearing the woodland. It is a keen coloniser of open

Tree-spotting

Hawthorn   **Midland Hawthorn**

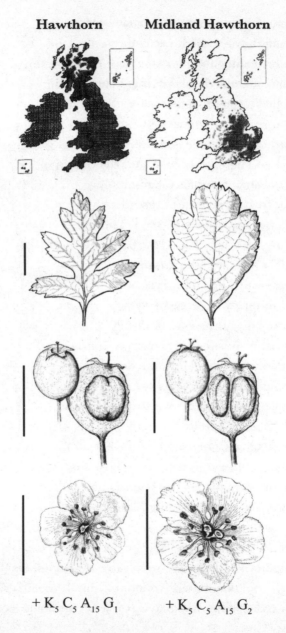

$+ K_5 \, C_5 \, A_{15} \, G_1$ $+ K_5 \, C_5 \, A_{15} \, G_2$

ground and, on account of its thorns, it is resistant to browsing. Large herbivores will browse, especially if pushed for fodder, but there comes a point when the reduced bushes become so compact that the density of thorns is prohibitive. Low bushes, in a heavily grazed state, persist around rabbit burrows, ready to resume normal growth again if grazing pressure eases.

Each *Crataegus* tree is self-incompatible – it needs to cross-pollinate. The species readily cross with each other, giving rise to many hybrids. On the continent, where there are several species, hybridisation can be very confusing. One sad long-term consequence of the compatibility between our two species is that Hawthorn is genetically more dominant and if our woodland habitat continues to contract, Midland Hawthorn will slowly be bred out of existence.

Hawthorn in particular becomes a mass of fruit in the autumn, hugely attractive to Blackbirds, Fieldfares, Blackcaps and Bullfinches. However, because the haws contain a mild toxin, only a small number are consumed each time by any individual, so the tree remains in fruit a surprisingly long time, providing a source of food all winter.

Many people dislike the smell of the flowers. Not surprising – the scent contains trimethylamine, which is also released from dead and rotting fish. Not surprising again then that flies are some of the keenest pollinators. The toxins in the haws also occur in the leaves and the bark and are there primarily to deter insect pests and fungal attack.

All members of the Rosaceae are rich in tannins and flavonoids, notably procyanidins. These chemicals have been used as traditional medicine for hundreds of years and for many complaints, notably various cardiovascular diseases.

There are no severe side effects and this usage is now supported by clinical data.

ROSACEAE

Rowan *Sorbus aucuparia*
Whitebeam *Sorbus aria*
Wild Service Tree *Sorbus torminalis*

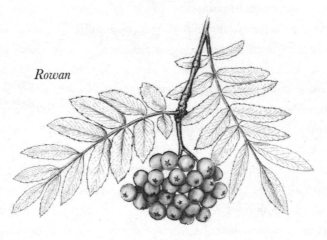

Rowan

If you are a hillwalking birdwatcher, you will associate Rowan with the Highlands and islands of Scotland – a lone windswept tree laden with 'berries', providing a rich feast for hordes of migrating Fieldfares after their flight south from the frozen north. Rowan's survival on exposed sites and at high altitudes prompted its other name, Mountain Ash. Despite arriving in Britain soon after the pioneers, around 11,000 BP, Rowan was not squeezed into the northern uplands by later species. It held its ground throughout the country. It is one of our most widespread trees, but it is not very common in any location. It is a light-demanding tree of rocky, well-drained sites and it avoids limey soils. On the continent, it is more common in the northern boreal forests of Europe than it is further south.

By complete contrast, Whitebeam waited until the climate was a lot warmer, around 7000 BP – too late to get across to Ireland … or did it manage? – we will see later. It failed to migrate naturally very far north, though it has been planted as an ornamental in parks and gardens, even on the Orkneys. It too thrives on well-drained soils but, unlike Rowan, it is closely associated with limey, rather than acid, soils.

It is not known exactly when Wild Service reached our shores, though it was probably late, along with Whitebeam, as there is no evidence it reached Ireland and the earliest record is of charcoal deposits dating from the Iron Age (long after we'd been separated from the continent). Like Whitebeam, it did not spread far northwards. A shade-tolerant species of clay soils that is seldom found naturally outside the woodland habitat, it is regarded as an indicator of ancient woodlands in the south.

Wild Service Tree

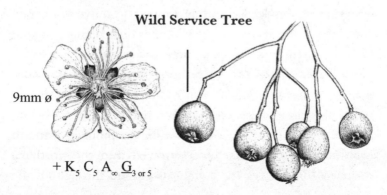

9mm ø

$+ K_5 \, C_5 \, A_\infty \, \underline{G}_{3 \text{ or } 5}$

Tree-spotting

All three *Sorbus* species are blessed with frothy, creamy-white inflorescences of small flowers tightly packed, each 80–200 flowers strong. They may look beautiful, but they carry a rather unpleasant smell, reminiscent of the trimethylamine of Hawthorn. The inflorescences develop into dense bunches of fruit, each similar in design to that of an apple, although much smaller with about 1cm diameter. The ovary walls do not become woody as in a a haw, but remain soft, as in an apple. The surrounding juicy hypanthium is bright red in Whitebeam and Rowan, but in Wild Service, pictured here, it is an unenticing speckled brown.

Sorbus is a curiously varied genus with regard to its leaf shape. As with all Rosaceae, they are arranged alternately, but some species have simple leaves like Whitebeam, some have lobed leaves like Wild Service and some have compound leaves, as in Rowan. Whitebeam leaves are thick, dark above and white-felted beneath, making them recognisable and a striking sight on a breezy day.

The pointed pinnate lobes of Wild Service are unlike those of any other lobed leaves. And few other native trees have compound leaves like Rowan. Elder and Ash have opposite leaves and fewer leaflets, while Rowan has alternate leaves with 11 to 19 leaflets.

The winter twigs of the three *Sorbus* species are easily distinguished. Both Whitebeam and Wild Service have green, hairless bud scales with brown edges, though the scales of the more pointed buds of Whitebeam have fringes of white hairs along the extreme edges. The bud scales of Rowan are brown with silky, appressed hairs scattered all over the surface, making it tricky to see the many scales.

Whitebeam   Wild Service   Rowan

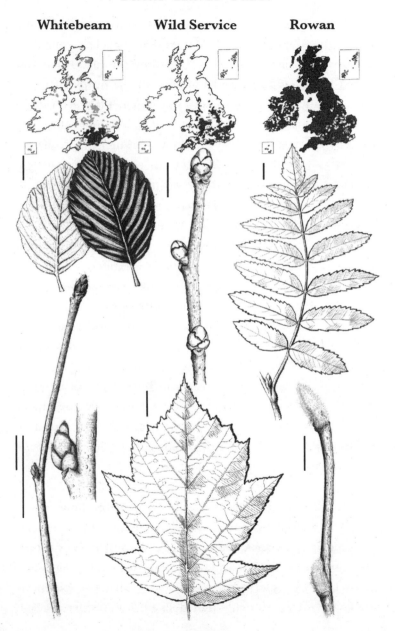

All *Sorbus* fruits are popular with a wide variety of birds and mammals. Those of Wild Service are best eaten by humans after they have 'bletted' – allowed to overripen and begun to decompose.. Conceptually, this is off-putting, but they actually taste rather good, like dates. They are rich in vitamin C and, carefully stored, were given to children as winter treats until the early twentieth century. The fruits are known as 'chequers' due to their speckled (chequerboard) appearance, and, before the wide use of hops, they were used to flavour beer or to make a liqueur, which is how the many 'Chequers Inns' got their name.

Rowan fruits contain carotenoids, citric acid, malic acid, parasorbic acid, pectin, provitamin A, sorbitol, tannin and vitamin C. (Note the two links to the genus *Sorbus* in the names of these chemicals.) From a human perspective this is a mix of healthy ingredients plus some that taste bitter and, in quantity, can upset the lining of the stomach or be toxic in other ways. Eating Rowan fruit fresh off the tree is not tempting. However, the bitter parasorbic acid, which causes indigestion and nausea, can be degraded and converted to the benign food preservative sorbic acid (note the link again) by freezing or cooking during the process of making excellent jams and chutneys, or a tea that wards off respiratory infections.

There is a complicated scientific story surrounding White-beam. It transpires that it is one of many similar species that superficially look indistinguishable and have a recent common ancestor. We call these microspecies. They arose in an unusual way referred to as apomixis – the development of viable seed from an ovule that does not require fertilisation by the male gamete from a pollen grain. There is no sharing and mixing of genes, so apomictically produced offspring are genetically identical to the parent plant in much the same way as new plants derived from cuttings or suckers.

It is probable that the original 'Whitebeam' was a variable species and was thinly scattered over a wide area. Each isolated plant was not able to cross-pollinate, but built up a local population of genetically identical individuals by apomixis. Each population was subsequently recognised as a microspecies, subtly but distinctly different from any other – for example, in the coarseness or fineness of the serrations along the leaf margins.

There are over 50 unique microspecies of Whitebeam in Europe. Most of our 26 have a westerly distribution, are extremely rare and each is confined to a limited area. They are particularly vulnerable to extinction because of their lack of genetic variation and their small populations. The most common microspecies is Whitebeam itself, *Sorbus aria*. It is regarded as the 'type species' with which all other Whitebeams are compared. We have the Hereford Whitebeam, Symonds Yat Whitebeam, Cheddar Whitebeam, Menai Whitebeam and Lancastrian Whitebeam, all of whose names reflect their limited location. Slightly less rare (in Ireland) is the Irish Whitebeam, *Sorbus hibernica* ... so Whitebeam did get to Ireland naturally after all!

RHAMNACEAE

Buckthorn *Rhamnus cathartica*
Alder Buckthorn *Frangula alnus*

Alder Buckthorn

These two Buckthorn shrubs are southerly species found growing together, especially in alkaline fenland marshes alongside willows and alders. They are shade-tolerant, so do well as an understory in wet woodland. However, Alder Buckthorn is also commonly found cheering up acid bogs with its vibrant-coloured berries, and Buckthorn occurs frequently in hedgerows on the chalk. Note that Sea Buckthorn, discussed next, belongs to a different family and very different habitat from those considered here.

Most members of the Rhamnaceae are small shrubs, seldom filling a dominant role in the landscape. Being mostly unpalatable, spiky and fire-resilient, they are strongly associated with Mediterranean climates. However, while both our species occur in the Mediterranean, they are never part of the dry, heavily grazed and fire-prone scrubby landscape known as garrigue. Instead, they grow better in deep shade and where the soil is moist and organically rich – maybe they were more common there in the past. The family characteristic of being unpalatable, and toxic in certain circumstances, is found in both our species. Only a few invertebrates actually seek out Buckthorn leaves – most famously, the Brimstone Butterfly, whose caterpillars will accept nothing else.

Unlike other families, the Rhamnaceae is undecided regarding opposite versus alternate leaf arrangement. Leaves of those in the genus *Rhamnus*, such as Buckthorn, are essentially opposite, though sometimes they are not precisely so. *Frangula* species, including Alder Buckthorn, have alternate leaves, though they occasionally manage to coincide in almost opposite pairs. You can use this 'indecisiveness' as an early clue to their identity. Both have simple leaves. Those of Buckthorn have finely and evenly serrated margins, while the margins of Alder Buckthorn leaves are entire. In both species the lateral veins of the leaves curve forward towards the tip of the leaf, instead of leading straight to the margin (a feature shared by Dogwood).

Their winter twigs are very different. Buckthorn has neat, dark buds on hairless twigs, which usually end in spines. In contrast, the buds of Alder Buckthorn have no bud scales, so look rather untidy on their hairy, spine-free twigs.

The creamy-green flowers of both are only 3mm to 4mm across. But they are clustered in groups, which makes them more obvious. Both provide easily accessible nectar, but do not attract a wide range of insects – mostly flies and beetles. Buckthorn is dioecious (although this is not obvious, because both male and female flowers retain vestigial organs of the other sex).

The fruits of both species are clusters of small, shiny, black drupes (around 8mm in diameter). Those of Alder Buckthorn are particularly attractive, as they start a pinky-yellow and change slowly to purply-black. Most shrubs carry all colour stages for some weeks during early autumn. The seeds are toxic to most mammals if consumed in quantity, but not to birds, who usually regurgitate them anyway.

The fruits of both buck-thorns were tradition-ally used in the production of the artist's pigment known as 'sap green', and the wood of Alder Buckthorn

Alder Buckthorn   **Buckthorn**

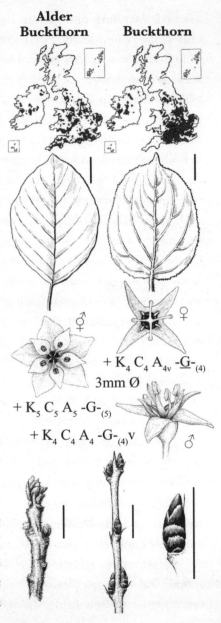

$+ K_4 C_4 A_{4v} -\underline{G}-_{(4)}$

3mm Ø

$+ K_5 C_5 A_5 -G-_{(5)}$

$+ K_4 C_4 A_4 -G-_{(4)}v$

is famed for being one of the best ingredients for making gunpowder. The steady burn rate of buckthorn charcoal made it ideal not just for the powder, but also particularly for its use as a time fuse.

Wicken Fen in Cambridgeshire is a tiny pocket of the once vast area of wetland – the Fens – which covered the lowlands of East Anglia adjacent to the Wash. Most of this area was drained for agriculture in the early nineteenth century. Only 1 per cent of the original wetland habitat remains today, and one key reason that Wicken Fen survived was because it provided a steady supply of buckthorn to the gunpowder industry.

Faversham in North Kent is regarded as the cradle of the British gunpowder industry. The site was perfectly surrounded by the willow and buckthorn thickets of the North Kent Marshes. In April 1916, this was the site of the worst explosion in the history of the British munitions industry; well over 100 people were killed.

ELAEAGNACEAE

Sea Buckthorn *Hippophae rhamnoides*

If your way to the sea across the sand dunes of eastern Britain is blocked by impenetrable, low-growing, spiny scrub with silvery leaves and wonderful, bright orange fruit, you have found Sea Buckthorn growing in its natural habitat. But you may already have become acquainted with it in your local supermarket car park. Its restricted natural distribution has been augmented by considerable amenity planting.

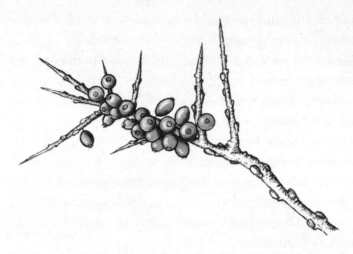

During the final phases of the Ice Age, Sea Buckthorn in its most stunted form was already playing a major role in the arctic tundra community that prevailed in southern Britain. It can grow to 11 metres in height, but in the cold, windswept or salt-sprayed habitats where it is typically found, it keeps a much lower profile.

The tundra soils of post-glacial landscapes, and indeed the pure sand of coastal dunes, are devoid of any available nutrients, notably nitrogen. Sea Buckthorn associates with a bacterium called *Frankia*, which helps it obtain nitrogen directly from the soil atmosphere, in much the same way as leguminous plants. But there are additional spin-offs from this association with *Frankia*. The bacterium provides more than enough nitrogen for the host plants' immediate needs. The excess is converted into nitric acid that is extruded into the surrounding soil, where it helps in the weathering of the bedrock, releasing other important nutrients tied up in the rock, notably phosphorus. This supports not only the buckthorn but also encourages the process of recolonization by other pioneer species.

As the ice retreated and the climate slowly warmed, Sea Buckthorn marched steadily onwards and its fibrous humus improved and enriched the tundra soils, enabling a succeeding wave of colonisers to follow on. But the low-growing tundra species eventually became overwhelmed by shade from the developing woodland canopies. Only those that kept ahead of the relentless march of vegetation survived. Dwarf Birch and the mat-forming willows with their interlocking branches retreated to the exposed tops of the higher mountains, where conditions were too severe for full-grown trees.

Sea Buckthorn chose a different inhospitable refuge – the windswept, shifting sand dunes along the coast. And here it has continued to thrive naturally in scattered, isolated sites along the east coast of Britain, where its fruits provide a welcoming winter feast for long-distance migrant birds which have battled their way to Britain above storm-tossed seas. The fruits are not only energy-packed with sugar, but they are also rich in minerals and vitamins. The Ancient Greeks fed it as a supplement to horses, giving rise to its name *Hippophae* – 'shining horse'.

This species is unlikely to be confused with any other native tree or shrub. The long, thin leaves, with entire margins, key out alongside Osier. But no willows are armed with spines like *Hippophae*. The only other heavily armed shrub that competes with *Hippophae* is Blackthorn. The bright orange 'berries' are not strictly berries but 'false' fruits – not unlike the haws of Hawthorns. The silver colour of the leaves is due to a coating of unusual stellate (star-like) hairs on both surfaces, particularly the lower. This is a characteristic feature of its family – Elaeagnaceae – which includes a number of garden shrubs and is loosely related to the other buckthorn family.

Due to its remarkable soil-binding ability, it has been planted (not always wisely) throughout Britain and other places round the world where habitat restoration requires a stabilising agent. But its rapid, vegetative spread often becomes invasive, smothering other native species. Invasiveness is not a prerogative of alien species. Some of our native species can be viewed as invasive even in their homeland, such as bracken in heathland and thistles in our back garden. In many other coastal sites around Britain, *Hippophae* has been planted to stabilise the dunes, but it has become a problem for other specialist sand-dune plant species. Even in its natural stronghold along the east coast of Britain, *Hippophae* is regarded as a pest. Most will have conservation

Sea Buckthorn

206

management programmes in place to control its spread and minimise its extent, though seldom with the aspiration of eradicating it all together. Its role as a refuge for migrating birds is too important.

It is the view of experts in the field that the 'invasive' behaviour of Sea Buckthorn is a result, as always, of human interference with the balance of nature. Around 2,000 years ago, large herbivores would have roamed freely and crashed their way through the *Hippophae* thickets, munching as they went. The dune systems would have been extensive and dynamic, with some thickets of *Hippophae* breaking up and giving way to open dunes, while other areas of bare sand would be colonised by dune species and gradually develop into dense *Hippophae* thickets.

My friend and colleague John McAllister tells me that, in the 1980s and 1990s, the Sea Buckthorn stands on the dunes at Sandwich Bay in Kent were subject to heavy defoliation on an annual basis by immense numbers of Brown-tail Moth caterpillars. The Buckthorn was stripped of its leaves each spring and summer. Miraculously, it survived this annual assault. However, its vigour was suppressed enough to prevent it extending its range as it does now. The Brown-tail Moth is still present, but not in the numbers it used to be. It is tempting to suspect this might be attributable to the wide use of pesticides. But entomologists tell us that the Brown-tail Moth populations have always fluctuated in response to the variations in numbers of a parasite whose activity, in turn, is controlled by a hyperparasite. So we really need to be looking at what might be affecting the hyperparasite.

ULMACEAE

Wych Elm *Ulmus glabra*
English Elm *Ulmus procera*
Field Elm *Ulmus minor*

Wych Elm in fruit

For tree lovers, particularly those of a certain age, one of the most tragic stories of the twentieth century was that of the elm. In the early 1970s I started teaching at Flatford Mill Field Centre on the Suffolk–Essex border – the heart of a landscape made famous by John Constable, whose sketches and masterpieces feature a majestic elm in nearly every scene. Elms continued to be a major, graceful and elegant feature of the rural landscape of lowland England and Wales until the mid 1970s, when the full impact of the tragic event was made glaringly evident. Thousands of mighty, lifeless skeletons stood out poignantly throughout the landscape – a heart-wrenching and constant reminder until they were felled and finally removed forever. I refer, of course, to Dutch elm disease (DED).

All three of our elms were affected, but the English Elm was hit worst of all. Its name suggests a thoroughly native species, but it is actually an archaeophyte, introduced to Britain possibly by the Romans but more likely by earlier migratory peoples. It did not spread naturally across to Ireland, but neither did it spread into northern England or beyond. Although it no longer graces our landscapes as one of our tallest and most beautiful trees, it has retained its former distribution as an undistinguished, suckering, hedgerow shrub, succumbing to DED every time it raises its head above the hedge top. It is a species that favours deep, moist soils, notably along river valleys.

Field Elm is possibly native but could equally be a Bronze Age archaeophyte with many distinct varieties that have been introduced from Europe over the subsequent centuries. In the past, botanists considered these varieties should be rated as fully legitimate species, but this view is no longer believed to be tenable. In fact, current thinking (based on genetics) is that English Elm might simply be one of these introduced varieties. Field Elm is a southern lowland species that, like English Elm, is seldom found as a tall tree nowadays. It occurs in hedgerows and wood margins, occasionally forming small copses but rarely in woodland.

Wych Elm is a true native that returned to Britain around 9,500 years ago along with the oaks, with which it faithfully associated until the first elm decline around 5000 BP. This decline coincided with Neolithic forest clearances. However, because the decline was abrupt and widespread and there was no bounceback as with other tree species, it was almost certainly due to another widespread pathogenic attack. But

Wych Elm did eventually recover and is now widespread in our islands, most abundant in the north and west – an oceanic species, the significance of which is covered on page 213. Its northern stronghold is beyond the worst ravages of DED. So here there are still some immensely tall trees surviving in mixed or pure woodland. It is also a tree of hedges, field borders and streamsides, and is a successful colonist of ungrazed grassland, rocky and waste ground, especially on base-rich soils.

DED entered Europe on Canadian elm logs. It is caused by a pathogenic fungus, *Ophiostoma novo-ulmi*, that is specific to elms and is carried by the Large Elm Bark Beetle, *Scolytus scolytus*, whose range does not currently stretch to northern Scotland. But with the climate warming, that may change. The beetle creates wonderfully patterned brood chambers under the bark of dead and dying elm wood. Hordes of young beetles emerge from these chambers and disperse to find live elm twigs upon which to feed, carrying the fungus with them. Elm shrubs that hunker down below the tops of the hedges usually escape notice and survive. As the young beetles burrow into the bark of young twigs to feed, they carry fungal spores into the trees' veins, from whence the fungus spreads to the rest of the tree. It interrupts the transportation of water and nutrients in the vascular tissue, leading eventually to the tree's demise. Collateral damage associated with DED includes the dramatic decline of the White-letter Hairstreak butterfly and the extinction in Britain of the Large Tortoiseshell butterfly, which depended upon the elm as its primary food plant. DED has also resulted in the increasing rarity of a number of nationally scarce species of lichens.

Despite the hybrids and the large number of introduced look-alike subspecies of Field Elm, probably the most commonly occurring elms are the three species considered here – and it is possible to distinguish between them. The leaves of all elms are simple, arranged alternately and have biserrated margins. Uniquely, the leaf blade is asymmetrically attached to the petiole, making the leaves lopsided, and distinct in this respect from all other trees.

The big ID problem these days is that most Field Elms (including English) survive as suckers in hedgerows, and the leaves of suckers are almost always atypical of the species. Wych Elm, too, is often found as regrowth from old stumps. What never fails is the lopsided base to the leaf blade, but this is easy to overlook. Most Field Elms, again including English, are clones derived from suckers and therefore have minimal genetic variation. This reduces the potential for DED resistance. Wych Elm does not sucker readily, but spreads by seed. This results in genetic variability and a degree of resistance but, long-term, it does not look promising. Conservationists are in three minds regarding a solution:

- isolate and nurture the surviving populations;

- let nature take its course;

- replace them with non-native, resistant species.

Much to my surprise, I find that I favour the third option. Despite the concern about potential 'invasive aliens', it seems like a good idea to fill as much as possible of the ecological

English Elm

Almost round
<1.5x as long as wide.
Roughly hairy on the
upper surface.

Field Elm

Typically 2x as long as wide
but very variable in length.
Typically hairless & shiny
on the upper surface.

Wych Elm

Obovate with 1–3 tips
< 2x as long as wide.
Roughly hairy on the upper
surface.

Corky ridges on 2-year-old
twigs, only on English Elm

English Elm is
similar but more hairy

Scattered orange hairs;
buds not central to leaf scars

niche and functions left vacant by the demise of the elms. Sycamore may be the most reliable candidate. This may be worth considering even more seriously in the upland Ash woods of Scotland, where both dominants, Wych Elm and Ash, are seriously threatened by introduced diseases.

English Elm is self-sterile and anyway neither it nor Field Elm are often seen in flower. But Wych Elm is capable of setting viable seed at a surprisingly young age (13 years), and when it flowers, it does so in great profusion.

Individually, each flower is small and petalless, but collectively, they put on an attractive show before the leaves burst. Soon they are replaced by translucent-winged, single-seeded fruits (often called samaras).

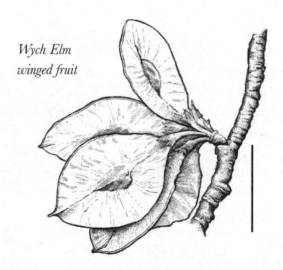

Wych Elm winged fruit

Before these fully ripen they are eagerly devoured by any finch that happens to be around. Those that are dispersed by the wind and fall to the ground need to germinate within a week or else they die – if they aren't consumed by rodents and ground-feeding birds first. Wood mice and sparrows are the keenest foragers. Elm leaves are much sought-after by many mammals and have been used as fodder for domestic animals for thousands of years.

Elm wood has long been the traditional wood for making coffins. Another little-known use of elm wood exploits its water-resistant properties. Hollowed-out elm trunks and branches were some of the first water pipes used in London in the thirteenth century. Between the sixteenth and eighteenth centuries, i.e. before widespread lead piping, all the main water pipes in London, for both water supply and sewage conveyance, were made from bored elm.

FAGACEAE – AN INTRODUCTION

Western Europe as far north as the British Isles can be considered the realm of the Fagaceae. Before Neolithic people started the ongoing process of forest clearance, the British Isles were swathed in oak woodland.

This is a bit sweeping, of course, because oak was often accompanied by other co-dominants, such as elm or lime. Most of the Central Highlands of Scotland were dominated by Scots Pine, while Black Poplar, Alder and willows held sway along the broad floodplains of many big rivers further south. Nevertheless, in general terms, the British Isles were, for thousands of years, dominated by oak forest. In fact, the family Fagaceae plays a disproportionately dominant role throughout western Europe.

Sessile and Pedunculate Oak are well-tuned to the

oceanic climate that prevails in Britain and extends down the western seaboard of Europe, from the north of Scotland to part way down the Iberian peninsula, where oceanic gives way to Mediterranean climate. The south-westerly winds, such a familiar feature of the British climate, bring wet weather that ameliorates the extremes of temperature experienced by countries in the heart of Europe at similar latitudes. Under the influence of the Atlantic, winters are cool, rarely bitterly cold, the summers are generally mild and warm, seldom overwhelmingly hot, and all seasons are characterised by being wet, unlike the much drier climates of inland Europe.

The woodlands along the extreme coastal fringes of this Atlantic belt not only receive the bulk of the rain but, between the showers, are exposed to daily sea mists and are classified as temperate rainforest. There are still remnants of these rainforests in Galicia (northwest Spain) and especially in western Britain – scattered gems occurring mostly on steep, inaccessible hillsides. Moss-covered rocky boulders, waterfalls and rushing streams are an integral part of the scene. These Atlantic oak woods, with their stunted and twisted oak trees and rich epiphytic flora, are recognised for their global uniqueness.

Inland from the coast, but still under the influence of the Atlantic, the deciduous oak woods are rather different – more majestic. These temperate oak forests were those that once dominated the rest of the British Isles, penetrated halfway across France from the Bay of Biscay, and created a broad belt along northern Spain, north of the sparsely wooded *dehesa* landscape of Spain's high tableland, where our oaks start to mingle with other deciduous and evergreen oak species.

Today our two deciduous oaks stretch eastwards as far as western Asia, but they cease to be the dominant species across the comparatively dry plains of central Europe, where the summer and winter temperatures are more extreme. This vast landscape was once the domain of the mighty Beech, *Fagus sylvatica*, also a member of Fagaceae. Beech is still a major presence in many of the remaining continental woodlands in the heart of Europe, where it is often co-dominant with Silver Fir (*Abies alba*).

South of the Beech forests of central Europe, the influence of the Mediterranean creates a climate of warm, wet winters and long, hot, dry summers. In the evergreen Mediterranean forest, called maquis, the Fagaceae still dominate – here, evergreen oaks once cloaked the sun-drenched hillsides, providing welcome shade in the summer and a sponge for the rain in winter. There are still remnants of maquis dominated by Cork Oak and Holm Oak, along with pines, the scrubby Kermes Oak and other aromatic maquis species. Sadly, most of this forest has now gone, leaving a very arid, inhospitable landscape which is severely eroded by the heavy winter downpours, now that there is no tree cover to hold the soils that absorb and retain the water.

At higher altitudes and on north-facing slopes, Sweet Chestnut (again from the Fagaceae) forms a transitionary belt, mixing with the evergreen oaks on the one side and coniferous forest, deciduous oaks and Beech on the other.

So without a doubt most of Europe was, and, where natural forest still survives, still is under the dominion of members of the Fagaceae. One reason for this dominance could be that the symbiotic EcM associations seem to be richer within the Fagaceae than with any other family of trees. The immense importance of these partnerships cannot be overstated. Not all trees are ectomycorrhizal, but those that are tend to be the major players in any temperate woodland community. In northern temperate regions EcM partnerships must give the host trees a competitive advantage. The competitive edge is enhanced by the leaf litter of the dominant trees, which saprophytic organisms find particularly hard to decompose, but which EcM fungi can break down with ease.

Another attribute that Fagaceae have in common, and which partly contributes to their success as dominant species in temperate regions, is wind pollination. This feature enabled them to spread beyond the tropical jungles to exploit the cooler, windswept lands where good pollinating insects are in comparatively short supply.

All members of the Fagaceae are woody plants with deciduous (or evergreen) alternate leaves. They all bear unisexual catkins, with both sexes occurring on the same plant (monoecious) and produce nuts that are supported or protected in a cupule (cup). The fruit and the form of this protective cupule is one easy way to tell the members of the Fagaceae apart – the oak has acorns in cups, whereas the nuts of Beech and Sweet Chestnut are fully encased, with the cupule of the Sweet Chestnut covered with spines. Minute inspection of the flowers of the female catkins reveals miniature versions of the fruit and cupules that follow.

The names Fagaceae and *Fagus* (Beech) come to us from the Greek *phagein*, meaning 'to eat'. Acorns, chestnuts and beech nuts are rich in protein, much-valued fodder not only for birds and mammals but also for humans throughout history – eaten whole or ground into flour. Many have been cultivated since ancient times. Sweet Chestnuts are still an economically important crop on the Continent, although susceptibility to the chestnut blight fungus has damaged the market. Although not a commercial crop, the acorns produced by most of the 500 species of *Quercus* (oaks) are edible, but many require some preparation to remove the tannins. Throughout the world, the acorns of several oak species are used as feed for livestock and are important to local wildlife populations. In Britain, jays in particular are renowned for their enthusiasm for acorns and for their role in dispersal.

All Fagaceae, especially oaks, are rich in tannin (a polyphenol). Tannin occurs in most plants except mosses, but usually in much lower quantities than in the Fagaceae. This chemical can be toxic to most animals, especially when consumed in high doses, but is beneficial in small amounts. It is commonly located in the thin, waxy coating of leaves, sometimes in specialised cells or in the cell vacuoles, where it can be isolated from most cellular functions. The bitterness of tannins (attributable particularly to esters of gallic acid and proanthocyanidin-type tannins) is highly effective in deterring excessive browsing. Foraging animals, such as pigs, that are capable of eating tannin-rich leaves, produce a salivary protein, mucin, that binds to the tannins and prevents them from being absorbed. Tannins also limit the activity of decomposer microorganisms of leaf litter (and hence, nutrient recycling) on the forest floor. This contributes to the sequestering of carbon, thus having implications for climate change. It also accounts for the deep and long-lasting layers of leaf litter in Beech and oak woods that are such fun in the autumn, and which provide precious bedding for hibernating hedgehogs.

Tannin from the inside of oak barrels adds to the astringent flavour of wine and the health benefits of the tannins of wine, tea and olive oil, etc., and of other polyphenols, are widely accepted. But so far they have proved extremely difficult to confirm scientifically. Tannins extracted from oak bark provided the foundation of the leather-tanning industry, although today, inorganic tanning agents account for 90 per cent of the world's leather production.

FAGACEAE

Beech *Fagus sylvatica*

I'm sure I'm not alone in choosing a particular Beech tree as my most favourite tree. My majestic specimen sits calmly in the middle of a beautiful mixed wood. Standing beneath it, gazing up its mighty trunk and through its strong branches, one is filled with a sense of awe and humility. It seems to have stood peacefully here forever, providing a haven for a myriad of creatures and a wealth of ectomycorrhizal toadstools.

Yet Beech was a reluctant latecomer to Britain, returning about 6000 BP, during the wet Atlantic period. It is more at home in the drier continental climates of central Europe than the wet oceanic climate of the British Isles. It does not usually compete successfully with oak in Britain except on the well-

drained limestone (chalky) uplands of the south. Botanists have yet to pronounce on its native range (hence there is no distinction on the map). It is hard to interpret the pollen record. The free-draining soils of limestone uplands are not well-endowed with lakes and lake sediments or with deep layers of peat. Also Beech pollen, which is never produced in abundance and is poorly designed aerodynamically, is not widely dispersed. Beech is unlikely to have spread naturally very far north or west of southeast Wales, although it has been planted as far north as the Orkneys.

In summer, Beech forests are cool and dark, because the uppermost leaves create a complete and uniform canopy. Only a few shade-tolerant species can thrive on the woodland floor, notably those that can take advantage of the winter and spring sunshine when the canopy has not developed. Yew, being evergreen, often occurs as a scattered understory

Beech

and, in the spring, before the canopy develops and the sun can still reach it, the forest floor is usually thickly carpeted with bluebells.

Beech leaves are alternate, simple and usually have an entire, undulating margin (sometimes serrated). They are about 1.5x as long as wide, and are most often confused with Hornbeam, which has a biserrate margin. The winter buds are particularly characteristic, being long and pointed and sticking out at a prominent angle from the stem.

The cupules of Beech are four-lobed, whiskery and woody, and completely envelop the two (or three) triangular nuts while they mature. They are not produced at all some years. As a result the natural predators of the nuts die out, move elsewhere or tick over in low numbers. Every five years or so, all the Beech trees in the forest synchronise in producing a bumper crop, at which point the guzzling hordes are at their lowest ebb and so most of the nuts escape predation and have a chance of germinating into new seedlings. The nuts are referred to as mast – so there are good and poor mast years. The same phenomenon occurs with oak trees.

The Anglo-Saxon name for Beech was *boc*, and present-day Germans call it *buche*. Both these words are close to the word 'book', or *buch* in German. It is believed that the smooth bark of Beech trees was used early on as a writing tablet – just as it is today by vandals who carve their names into the smooth trunk.

FAGACEAE

Sweet Chestnut *Castanea sativa*

In the Bennett household, Christmas is a season synonymous with the Sweet Chestnut. At this time of year, we make chestnut stuffing, chestnut soup and chestnut bourguignon, or we roast them in the evenings over an open fire. Sweet chestnuts are high in protein, relatively low in fat, higher in starch than a potato, and the only nut to contain vitamin C.

Our prehistoric ancestors would not have had these benefits because the warmth-demanding Sweet Chestnut is not a voluntary coloniser of the British Isles. Its natural range is southern Europe and southwest Asia. It was generally believed to have been introduced by the Romans, but the evidence for this is based only on remnants of wood associated with archaeological sites. There has been no convincing palynological evidence. The oldest reliable record is a written one dated 1113. During medieval times it became a popular tree for parks and gardens, as well as for coppice plantations, where it is normally cut on a 15-year rotation. It does not grow freely in the wild. It thrives best on well-drained acidic soils in the southeast of England and East Anglia – where the rainfall is lowest, the summers are warmest and, incidentally where, because it has been planted as a crop, it is more commonly found than any native tree. Many of the coppice plantations are centuries old and feel like ancient woodland. This species is a relative newcomer to Britain therefore it has not had time to build up the same wealth of associations with other living organisms as have the oaks or Beech. It supports an embarrassingly low variety of wildlife; however, the habitats developed by traditional coppice management compensate for this.

Coppice management, now mostly for fencing materials, ensures the greatest diversity of habitat and a remarkably diverse community. Middle-aged coppice stands provide dense cover for nesting nightingales; relatively old and tall stands of trees cast dense shade in summer, but allow anemones and bluebells in the spring, while more recently coppiced stands and the sunny open rides are haunted by White Admirals, Fritillaries and other butterflies in the summer.

Sweet Chestnut

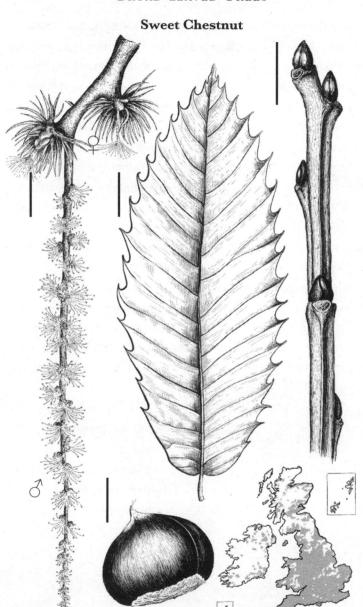

The trunk is fissured vertically and markedly, and distinctly twisted. This feature is discernible only in large, mature specimens so is seldom useful for identification. But Sweet Chestnut has a couple of other unique features: the glossy nuts concealed by a wickedly spine-covered cupule and large, simple leaves with clearly serrated margins. The serrations coincide with, and only with, the tips of the lateral veins. The serrations of no other tree leaf in Britain behave like this. The winter buds are small, with only two bud scales, and are borne on twigs that are often boldly ridged.

The flowers, although borne in catkins, are insect-pollinated like those of willows, and provide bees with valuable nectar as well as copious pollen. The catkins develop in early summer once the leaves have opened. After pollination you can often find the long male catkins littering the ground beneath the trees like pipe cleaners, followed in autumn by the plump nuts, usually (and frustratingly) still hidden in their spiny cupules.

FAGACEAE

Sessile Oak *Quercus petraea*
Pedunculate Oak *Quercus robur*

Pedunculate Oak

'Mighty oaks from little acorns grow.'

This fourteenth-century proverb (possibly a misquote from Chaucer) has much significance to many aspects of our everyday lives. It inspires us never to give up, and to remember that great things come from small beginnings. Oak leaves and acorns are used as symbols of aspiration by many organisations and indeed whole nations. While this lesson of perseverance and strength could be drawn from many trees, the supremacy of the oaks was probably already thoroughly embedded in the psyche of prehistoric 'Brits'. Oak trees had returned to lowland Britain by 9000 BP. Spreading northwards, they gradually established their dominance across most of our islands, forming mixed oak forest. On account of their longevity, they stood for resilience, and in the eyes of those, past and present, who sense an element of spirituality in the natural world, the oak stands for the additional virtues of patience and wisdom.

But 'oak' in Britain is in fact two different species. The distribution of both is widespread (avoiding only the highest and most northern locations) but in practice, Pedunculate Oak chooses heavy, fertile, clay soils, especially in the drier south and east where they don't get waterlogged, while Sessile Oak prefers better-drained, acid soils, so thrives best in the north and west, where there is plenty of rainfall. In upland oak forest, Sessile is the dominant of the two. Well-drained soils in the east suffer from drought, whereas the heavier soils retain moisture for longer. These differences are only partly reflected in the maps, which indicate presence and absence – not abundance – in each 10km by 10km square.

The female flowers and acorns of Pedunculate Oak are borne well clear of the developing leaves, on a long stalk or peduncle, while those of Sessile Oak are stalkless, sessile, and half hidden by the young leaves. The opposite is true of the leaves: Sessile Oak has a long-stalked leaf, whereas Pedunculate Oak leaves are almost sessile.

The winter buds are clustered at the tips of the twigs, a key feature of both species, and have numerous bud scales, fewer than 20 in Pedunculate, and more than 20 in Sessile. But be aware that the hybrid between them, *Quercus x rosacea*, is common and exhibits intermediates in all these features. The terminal buds give rise to a bunch of twigs all sprouting from almost the same point. Stand back and you can see this growth pattern reflected in the way that the main branches diverge, and how this gives the oak its characteristic sturdy, bushy silhouette.

Broad-leaved Trees

Pedunculate Oak   Sessile Oak

In addition to our native oaks, there are a number of introduced species, such as the Red Oak and Holm Oak, but these are usually planted for ornamental purposes and are not normally found in abundance in the wild in the British Isles. An exception is Turkey Oak, which grows like a weed in Kent – literally. It springs up along the edges of cornfields, immediately after harvesting.

Despite their strong tannin content, it seems that both our oaks support a greater diversity of wildlife than any of our other native species. As a result, oaks have attracted considerable entomological research, and so their prowess in this regard may be slightly exaggerated. Oaks and other native trees have been around for a very long time. Also oaks have, of course, been the most dominant for a long time, which has given them greater opportunity to build associations with many other species of wildlife. They are remarkably tolerant of being stripped of their leaves when insect numbers surge, and can produce a second flush of leaves if necessary.

The variety of both EcM toadstools and different galls found on oaks is testament to the popularity of the species with fungi and with gall-forming insects and mites. Galls are formed when, for example, a gall-forming insect lays its eggs into the tissue of the plant, mostly in the leaves or flower buds. The damage caused by egg-laying triggers the tree to create a characteristic growth, the gall, around the egg.[13] The gall provides protection and plentiful food for the developing grub when it hatches. Familiar types of galls include

---

13 Galls can be triggered not only by insects and mites but also by nematodes, fungi, bacteria and viruses.

spangle galls, cherry galls, currant galls, knopper galls, as well as the versatile oak apple, which was used in the past for making an indelible ink – a mixture of crushed oak apples with an iron sulphate solution. The mixing of iron with oak tannins, conveniently present in the easily collectable galls, makes the ink permanent.

Of the over 400 invertebrate species associated with oak, we have room to focus only on one, the Purple Hairstreak butterfly, which lays its eggs at the base of oak buds that are exposed to the sun in high summer. But instead of choosing an exposed, lone oak, the adult prefers the more sheltered conditions provided by the woodland habitat. As a result, the Purple Hairstreak is not an easy butterfly to spot, yet in suitable woods, especially in southern Britain, there may be hundreds of them perched out of sight on the top of the oak canopy – not deliberately reclusive but, like so much of our wildlife, easily overlooked unless you search for it.

There is nothing to compare with an oak wood in spring. The melody of birdsong, the hum of insects and the colourful carpets of bluebells and other wildflowers combine to create something unique, which indeed it is. Globally, these bluebell woodlands are restricted to a narrow corridor in northwest Europe, and are at their finest in the British Isles. We should not take this extraordinary privilege for granted.

Oak timber is extremely strong, hard, waterproof and resistant to warping, making it perfect for seafaring craft. Viking longboats were made with oak, and so too were the warships of the British Navy, before metal was preferred. The structural frameworks of large barns, grand houses and cathedral roofs were constructed with oak. High levels of tannin and other polyphenols in oak timber can explain its natural resistance to rot. The popularity and availability of oak over time resulted in massive harvesting of the biggest and best, leading to a decline in the quality of the gene pool for the 'biggest and best'. So sadly, the 'mighty' oaks of today are undoubtedly poor representatives of those that reigned in their former grandeur.

BETULACEAE – AN INTRODUCTION

Members of the Betulaceae – Birch, Alder, Hazel and Hornbeam – play a major role in the natural forests of the British Isles, often forming the dominant species. Like Salicaceae and Fagaceae, all Betulaceae are ectomycorrhizal, so after the ice retreated, they had a big advantage in the early colonisation of our islands. Despite seeming so delicate, the elegant yet hardy Birches, being wind-dispersed, were the first trees to arrive. Their fungal partners helped them not only to survive but also to thrive as the dominant tree for over a thousand years, forming open, sunny woodlands.

Pioneers aren't simply the first to explore and settle a new area, they are the ones who help prepare the way for others to follow. In the case of the pioneering Birch, the fungal network was fundamental in helping them support other mycorrhizal newcomers. Alder colonised the wetter hollows and valley bottoms, eventually forming impenetrable swamps, while Hazel, which takes longer to spread, eventually took over as the most widespread woodland type – until oak and others took over in their turn, leaving Hazel to dominate the understory and woodland edges. Hornbeam, preferring a warmer, drier climate, arrived later and was not so enthusiastic about spreading very far north or west. It is a beautiful addition to any wood but seldom found naturally as the dominant species.

All four are wind-pollinated and bear catkins – male and female on the same tree (monoecious). Birch produces numerous, tiny, winged, single-seeded fruits that are dispersed widely helping the species to spread rapidly into uncharted territory. Hornbeam and Alder fruits are also single-seeded and carried by wind. Meanwhile, Alder can also be dispersed by water because its fruit wall is corky and designed to float. Hazel is different – the female flowers develop into large nutritious nuts that are devoured, and dispersed especially by squirrels and jays.

All have simple, alternate leaves with a characteristically biserrate margin – except for Downy Birch, which has a more uniformly serrate margin.

BETULACEAE

Silver Birch *Betula pendula*
Downy Birch *Betula pubescens*

Birches are the trailblazers across any open or disturbed ground, particularly that which is acid. Both species occur throughout Britain, with Downy Birch favouring the wetter soils. It is the hardier of the two, often forming the upland woodland in northern Britain and Ireland and is especially associated with Eared Willow scrub, on the fringes of acid bogs.

Silver Birch

Meanwhile, Silver Birch occurs on the well-drained, acid soils of sandy heaths, especially in the southern lowlands.

Silver Birch is renowned for its 'silver' bark and its graceful, pendulous branches. Downy Birch points its twigs to the sky and also has white bark, though it is less brilliant and often obscured by a haze of browny-green algae, owing to the dampness of its preferred habitat. Downy Birch does not share the characteristic black gashes that occur at the base of the trunks of mature Silver Birch. Instead, it is smooth to the ground. Young trees take time to develop these more obvious distinguishing features, but are easily told apart in other ways.

Silver Birch mature trunk

Downy Birch twigs are dull and softly hairy, while Silver Birch twigs are hairless, shiny and dotted with pale 'warts'. Use a lens. Birch buds are slender and pointed. Male catkins form, usually in pairs, at the tips of the twigs before the leaves fall in autumn, but they remain dormant until April or May, when the smaller, upturned, female catkins form. By autumn the female catkins hang down, heavy with scores of tiny fruit. If you break one up, you will find the winged fruits and their fleur-de-lis-shaped bracts.

A typical Silver Birch leaf is shaped like an ace of spades, while Downy Birch leaves are egg-shaped. In practice, both species are very variable in leaf characteristics, and they are often tricky to identify with certainty. They do hybridise, but the hybrid is not thought to be that common, despite considerable overlap in their distribution.

Birch woods are enchanting habitats with a diverse and colourful ground flora, which is due to their open canopies that allow plenty of light to reach the forest floor. The foliage is palatable and enjoyed by many invertebrates. In addition to a wealth of toadstools that arise from the ectomycorrhizal fungi, dead wood is quickly rotted by many saprophytic species. Some of the birchwood insects and fungi produce galls, such as witches' brooms – dense masses of stunted twigs crowded together. They can often be seen on the high branches of birch trees, and look like mistletoe or birds' nests. This particular gall is triggered by a parasitic fungus called *Taphrina betulina*.

Besoms are traditional brooms constructed from a bundle of twigs tied to a stout pole. One of the most famous besom broomsticks is a flying version that belongs to Harry Potter. His 'Firebolt' is made from a bundle of Birch twigs tied to an Ash pole handle.

Birch bark is versatile and has been used for millennia for countless purposes. Removing bark from any living tree almost always kills the tree. Only the extreme outer papery film can be safely removed – but this has limited value on its own, except perhaps as a form of 'paper'.

The bark contains betulin, a triterpene which has fungicidal properties and is also responsible for giving the bark its white colour. This whiteness may protect the tree from UV damage, enabling birches of the northern boreal forests to cope with the relentless exposure during the long hours of sunlight of the Arctic summers. Exciting medical research is finding that betulin causes some types of tumour cells to start a process of self-destruction. It has also been shown to reduce the size and improve the stability of atherosclerotic plaques, which, in turn, could have the potential to reduce the risk of heart attacks and strokes.

Silver Birch   **Downy Birch**

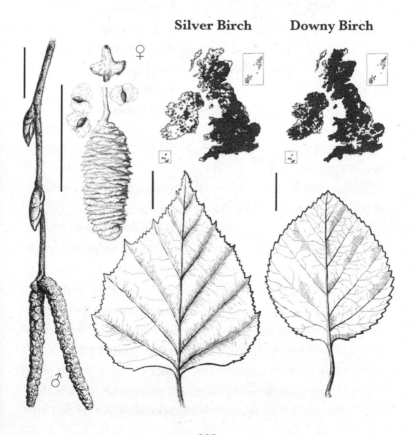

BETULACEAE

Alder *Alnus glutinosa*

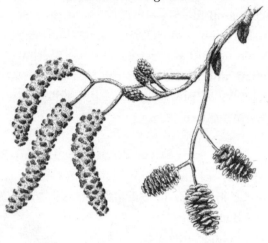

Alder forms the framework of probably the most secluded and inaccessible wildlife habitat in Britain – alder swamp.

Isolated Alder trees can be found alongside many streams and rivers throughout Britain, especially where the geology is moderately base-rich. Sadly, the glorious and extensive alder swamp that once filled many lowland floodplains is now a rare habitat, making it all the more precious. The valley floor is typically buried in really deep fluid peat derived from many generations of crowded stands of massive tussock sedges. Mildly enriched minor streams wind their way across the wetland. Alders first settle around the edges and disperse their seeds across the sedge swamp. Those that fall into the crowns of the scdges fare best. As the saplings grow and mature, their increasing weight causes the tussocks to sink and topple over, carrying the Alder trees with them. Side branches become new trunks and new shoots sprout from the old trunks, creating a tangled jungle. Progress across the swamp-filled valley by any means is not only dangerous but nigh impossible. I speak from experience – put a foot wrong and you get sucked into the mire. This is an unfamiliar and panic-inducing experience that seems to defy the laws of physics. Sadly for wildlife and carbon sequestration, most of these fantastic habitats have been drained to make way for agricultural activities on the fertile peat.

Alder played an important part in colonising the wet hollows in the lowlands of the thawing tundra landscape. As with Sea Buckthorn, its relationship with the bacterium *Frankia* gave it a huge advantage in a nutrient-poor landscape. When other species moved in, especially in slightly drier places, not only was the soil improved for them by Alder but they were also received 'with open arms', because, of course, Alder is mycorrhizal. Many different mycorrhizal toadstools are found in Alder woodland – several of them found only in association with Alder trees.

Mature Alder trees can be easily identified by the presence of Alder cones, which persist on the branches long after the tiny fruits have been shed and new green cones have started to form. Note that Alder cones are not equivalent to the cones of conifer trees; the woody bracts are not reproductive tissue and do not carry seeds. Instead, they support the tiny female flowers, each of which produces a single-seeded, corky-walled achene. The male catkins burst early and are some of the most attractive of all our catkin-bearing trees.

Alder

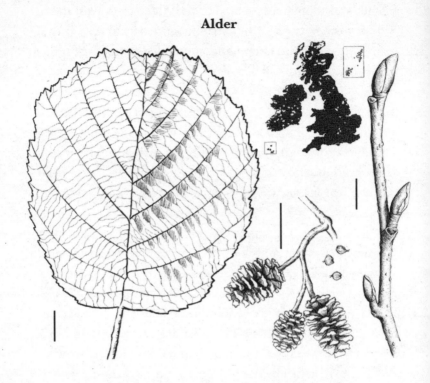

Alder's winter buds have two deep-mauve bud scales and uniquely stand on their own little shoots. The almost round leaves have a characteristic indented tip and the typical Betulaceae biserrate margin.

Unsurprisingly, Alder timber is durable under water and was used for the deep foundations of buildings, notably large medieval cathedrals. It was used from Neolithic through to Anglo-Saxon times to build causeways, such as those that crossed the Fenland marshes to the Isle of Ely. Today, Alder timber is deployed to reinforce river embankments in flood prevention schemes.

BETULACEAE

Hazel *Corylus avellana*

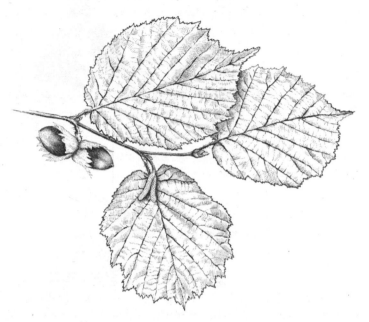

In Norse mythology, Hazel was known as the Tree of Knowledge. The Celts considered Hazel to be the source of wisdom, knowledge and heightened awareness. Traditional Chinese medicine, still practised today, regards Hazel as beneficial for the brain, and western nutritionists of the twenty-first century recognise that hazelnuts are especially rich in high levels of vitamin E, manganese, thiamine, folate and fatty acids, all of which promote nerve health and brain function. The ancients knew a thing or two.

Although not a pioneer, Hazel was an early coloniser of Britain – what a godsend for aspiring Mesolithic vegans

– and it featured strongly and uninterrupted in the pollen record thereafter. Nowadays, it occurs throughout the British Isles, from hedgerows to exposed cliff faces and as a shade-tolerant undershrub of many woodland types. As a result, it has been widely exploited throughout history, not just for its highly nutritious nuts but also for its versatile timber. Hazel has been the quintessential coppice species for centuries. For maximum return, Hazel is coppiced on a 7–10-year cycle. The most frequent traditional use for thinner and younger (or split) poles would have been for wattle and daub and for runners and spars in thatching. Coppice management for conservation is still practised in the southern lowlands of Britain. A familiar woodland type of oak standards (uncut, single-trunked trees) scattered amongst Hazel coppice, supports one of the richest carpets of spring flowers of any woodland. One of our best-loved mammals, the dormouse, is another fan of the dense growth of Hazel coppice and hedgerows. Here they find a perfect source of food and shelter to sustain them through their winter hibernation.

Hazel leaves are alternate, simple and almost round with a tapering tip and a heart-shaped base. Their margins are biserrate, typical of the Betulaceae. The leaves and the twig are hairy and the hairs are gland-tipped – a tiny, sticky blob that glistens red in early summer and discourages grazing insect larvae (use a lens – they are beautiful).

The winter buds are rounded and slightly flattened laterally. Male catkins form before the leaves fall in autumn, but they remain dormant until February or March, when the female catkins open. The nuts, with their thick, woody shells, ripen during September – if the squirrels don't get them first.

Sheep-grazed hazelnut plats (orchards) are a special feature of the Kent landscape, giving rise to a number of village names. The Kentish Cobnut, the most popular cultivated form of Hazel, originated here. Sadly, there are few working plats left today.

Hazel

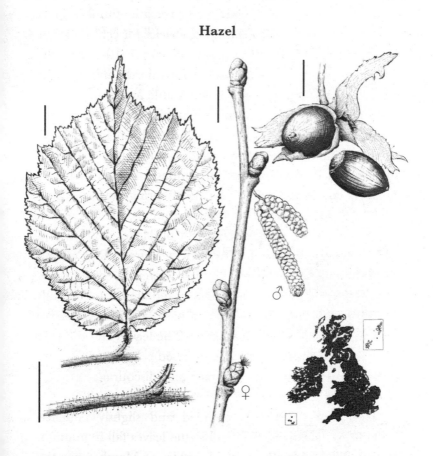

All you can see of the female catkin is the tiny tuft of bright red stigmas

243

BETULACEAE

Hornbeam *Carpinus betulus*

Oliver Rackham said, 'Hornbeam is the least documented of common trees ... it does nothing that other species will not do as well.' But I should like to write in praise of Hornbeam. It is a firm family favourite. Its stout, fluted and buttressed trunk, dappled sunlight in spring and translucent catkins bring its own unique and glorious character to our southern woods.

Hornbeam occurs commonly as part of the EcM community of many mixed oak forests growing on the clay soils in the south of Britain. It is not a northerner and is susceptible to late frosts, often failing to fruit after a cold spring. Although taller than some of its brethren in its family, Betulaceae, and rising above the understory in a wood, it is not as tall as oak or Beech, so it is seldom found as the natural dominant species. However, some woodlands became 'Hornbeam woods' under human influence from before the Iron Age, around 3000 BP, when its excellent potential as firewood was realised. It is resilient to repeated coppicing and pollarding, which became a form of management that provided a continuous supply of fuel.

Hornbeam is sometimes confused with Beech and elm because they have similar leaf shapes. But Beech leaves usually have entire leaf margins and elms have the distinctive asymmetrical attachment of the leaf bases. The biserrate margin and pleated look of Hornbeam leaves are characteristic. Also, Beech buds, though similar to those of Hornbeam, are longer, thinner and never appressed. The nutlets are attached to a unique pagoda-shaped bract that assists limited wind dispersal.

Hornbeam

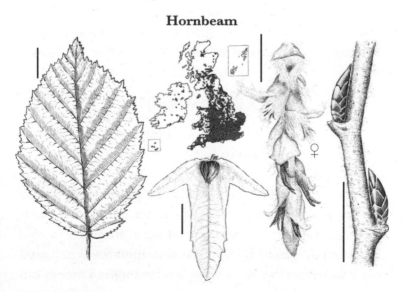

Many woodlands in the Weald are artificially dominated by Hornbeam. Over the centuries, oak and lime were steadily eliminated, while Hornbeam was selected and nurtured simply to provide a regular supply of charcoal for the local iron industry. The charcoal was made for centuries using the traditional 'mound method'. A large pile of wood was completely covered in earth before lighting and allowed to smoulder slowly. By limiting the amount of oxygen, the heat was sufficient only to drive off the water and sap and to chemically decompose the wood (driving off flammable gases), leaving pure carbon in the form of charcoal. Charcoal burns a lot hotter than wood, and without flame or smoke. Hornbeam wood is extremely hard (second only to Box) and produces charcoal that burns at the really high temperatures that are vital for smelting iron. The Wealden Hornbeam woods fuelled Britain's major iron industry from the Iron Age right through to the Industrial Revolution in the late eighteenth century, when coke replaced Hornbeam and the industry moved nearer to the coalfields of northern Britain.

SAPINDACEAE

Field Maple *Acer campestre*
Sycamore *Acer pseudoplatanus*

The maples that flank the eastern seaboards of the North American and the Asian continents put on world-famous autumnal displays of purples, reds, oranges and gold. Our own Field Maple, with its brilliant yellow autumnal foliage, could compete well on that stage. However, Sycamore (a widespread

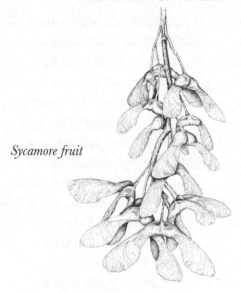

Sycamore fruit

non-native maple from mainland Europe) shuns flamboyancy – it often sheds its leaves while still green.

We'd urge you to lie quietly under a Sycamore tree in early summer, bathe in the delicate green shade and listen to the hum of thousands of bees and other insects foraging for nectar and sugary sap in the canopy. Once you tune in, the noise is almost deafening. Look at the flowers that grow in chains and see how the nectar glistens. What Sycamore lacks in variety of associated wildlife, it makes up for in numbers.

There is only one native *Acer* in Britain. Field Maple is a southerner that arrived too late after the Ice Age to get across to Ireland and chose to avoid the cooler and wetter north and west. It has since become a regular component of most mixed oak forests, especially in the south and east. Sycamore, on the other hand, is a robust opportunist that arrived much later, around 1500. Tolerant of wind, urban pollution, salt spray, and cold, wet winters, it now occurs in more parts of the British Isles than any other tree. It quickly invades open and disturbed ground, and is a successful competitor in most habitats. Understandably, it has acquired the reputation of being an aggressive weed.

Sycamore

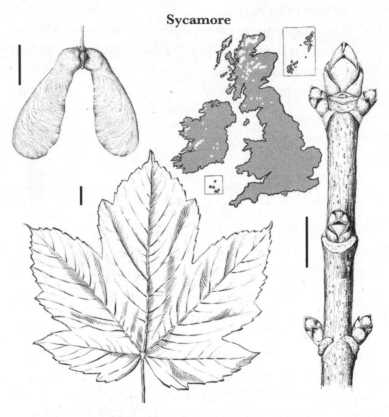

All maple leaves and buds are arranged in opposite pairs. They are easily recognised by their characteristic palmate leaf shape and their 'helicopter' fruits (pairs of single-seeded, winged and wind-dispersed nutlets).

Our two species are easily distinguished – check out the orientation of the fruit wings and the margins of the leaves. The winter twigs are markedly different too. The stout buds of Sycamore have green, black-edged scales and are hairless, while the smaller brown buds of Field Maple are covered in hairs.

Field Maple bears erect racemes of about 10 flowers. Sycamore has dangling panicles of about 30–60 flowers. All flower parts are yellow-green. Copious nectar is secreted from the basal disc in the centre of each flower.

Field Maple

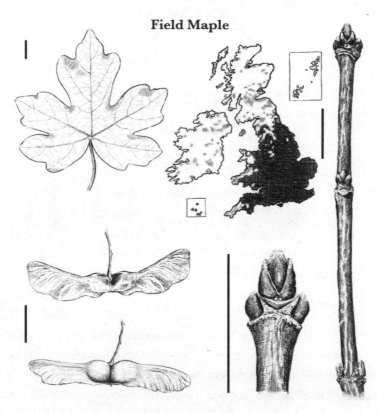

Our maples produce three different flower types: male, female and hermaphrodite. Within a single raceme of flowers, they may be: all male, all female, a mixture of males and females, or a mixture of males, females and hermaphrodite flowers. Importantly, the racemes of any one tree all bear the same combination of flower types, so the whole tree can be male, female or hermaphrodite. Where there is a mixture, the stamens mature before the stigmas are receptive, thus favouring cross-pollination.

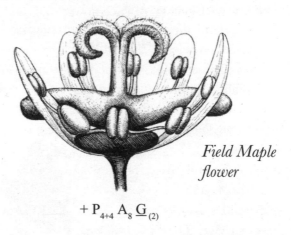

Field Maple flower

$$+ P_{4+4} \ A_8 \ \underline{G}_{(2)}$$

Even at the flowering stage the tiny wings of the fruit can be seen. The flower illustrated looks hermaphrodite but might be functionally female as the stamens are too short and therefore sterile. A high proportion of Sycamore trees that bear hermaphrodite flowers turn out to be functionally male, such that the female organs never form fertile fruit.

The sap of the Sugar Maple – and of all maples – can be tapped and turned into syrups or wines (though you need an awful lot of sap). As a recent non-native, Sycamore does not support a highly diverse fauna, but some leaf-grazing insects, notably aphids, gorge on the sap sugars and exude the excess in large quantities that drip from the leaves and coat anything below with a sticky film of 'honeydew'.

Maples have their own arbuscular mycorrhizal network which, although not as efficient on poor soils as EcM, works well on the nitrogen-rich soils the maples prefer. Maples are not ectomycorrhizal. They cannot rely on the cooperative support of other tree species in the EcM club. So they behave more aggressively – allelopathically – (Sycamore in particular) in order to defend their patch. Decomposing pigments of fallen maple leaves release chemicals that are toxic to other plant species. These toxins and the tree's notoriously dense shade inevitably suppress other plants to the extent that Sycamore is regarded as highly undesirable – not only in shedding 'honeydew', but also in threatening our native flora on a wide scale.

But the beautiful Sycamore tree does provide copious nectar for huge numbers (though not a great variety) of insects. Consider also its tenacity in the uplands where few other trees survive. The shelter it provides on a windswept, rain-drenched hillside must be welcomed by more creatures than just the ill-prepared hillwalker. Of course, we don't champion the aggressive nature of the species, but we do believe that the individual trees should be appreciated for their positive roles.

Since there are male and female trees (see opposite), it should be possible to thin out the female trees (so reducing further spread) and leave the male trees to provide nectar and, incidentally, an economic crop of timber. Male Sycamore trees grow faster and stronger than females by 10 per cent. One day we may be grateful to Sycamore. It is the most reliable contender to replace our fast-disappearing Ash trees. Not ideal but it may turn out to be the only way to sustain a bit of woodland continuity.

MALVACEAE

Large-leaved Lime *Tilia platyphyllos*
Lime *Tilia x europaea*
Small-leaved Lime *Tilia cordata*

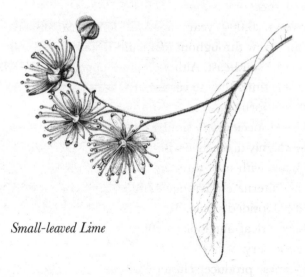

Small-leaved Lime

We have three species of lime; one of which, 'Lime', is a hybrid between the other two. It is extremely rare as a wild-growing tree and is almost certainly not of native origin. However, it is the most widely and commonly planted of the three, characteristically grown in long avenues through parkland, its lower trunks hidden by a thick mass of side shoots (epicormic growth) and its upper branches often festooned with Mistletoe. Its two parent species are not so widespread. Large-leaved Lime is rare in the wild, found locally in ancient woodland, typically on steep limestone terrain. But again, it is often planted for amenity and commercial purposes. Small-leaved Lime is more widespread, naturally occurring in mixed woodland on a wide range of soil types, but, despite often overtopping other trees, it never fills a dominant role. It is more abundant in the extreme climates of the south and east, barely extending into Scotland.

However, 6,000 years ago, all limes, Small-leaved in particular, grew throughout mainland Britain and dominated much of the southeast. Although limes penetrated the milder west at this time, they never reached Ireland – the Irish Sea had already formed.

All three species have similar features. In winter the zigzag twigs are highly distinctive with their (often wine-red) 'boxing-glove' buds, with two, three or occasionally four scales. The leaves are alternately arranged and easily recognised by their invariably lopsided shape. To distinguish the species, refer to the table overleaf and look carefully at the features with a lens where necessary.

All limes produce clusters of creamy-yellow flowers attached to a distinctive, long oblong bract. Each flower has a heavenly scent and produces copious nectar, much sought-after by bees and by moths at night. Lime honey has been an important product since prehistoric times.

The flowers of Small-leaved Lime attract the greatest

	Small-leaved Lime	Lime	Large-leaved Lime
Bud size	4–7mm	7–9mm	7–9mm
Twigs	Hairless	Hairless	Hairy
Leaf size	3–7mm	6–10cm	6–10cm
Leaf hairs underside	Orange tufts in vein angles	White tufts in vein angles	White, sparse & scattered
Flower clusters	Upturned	Pendulous	Pendulous
Epicormic growth on trunk	None	Abundant	None

variety of insects, but Large-leaved Lime's blooms provide the richest source of nectar. Because of this, the latter was planted for honey widely beyond its natural range throughout the monastic period and again later, since the mid seventeenth century, alongside Lime.

Among the cocktail of chemicals that contribute to the heavenly scent of the flowers is farnesol, a type of sesquiterpene that acts as a pheromone to attract pollinating insects. It is also antibacterial and deters mites. Present in the essential oils of many other flowers, it is used in perfumery to emphasize the odours by acting as a co-solvent that regulates the volatility of the odorants. It is also employed as a deodorant in cosmetic products because of its antibacterial activity. An infusion of the dried flowers of mostly Large-leaved Lime has long been regarded as soothing and medically beneficial.

The ovary of the flower has five chambers, each with several ovules, but the developing fruit, a nut, contains only one or two tiny viable seeds in total. These are highly nutritious and protected by a thick, woody and unpalatable fruit wall, making the seeds accessible only to Nuthatches and rodents. The nuts are small and the bract that remains attached is capable of carrying them several hundreds of metres in strong winds. Those that fail to get dispersed this way fall to the ground beneath the tree, where the seeds provide valuable winter food for small rodents.

Small-leaved Lime

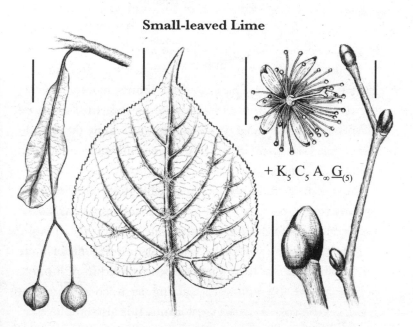

$$+ K_5 \, C_5 \, A_\infty \, \underline{G}_{(5)}$$

Limes are deep-rooted and drought-resistant. They are also ectomycorrhizal, like the pine, willow, oak and birch families, but unlike the rest of the Malvaceae. This explains their stable coexistence in mixed woodland and their period of dominance once the climate changed in their favour, around 6000 BP.

All lime species have been valuable economically. Before the advent of artificial fibres in the twentieth century, mankind relied entirely on natural fibres. All plants contain fibres, which are composed of cellulose. They serve many functions often associated with protecting the plant from physical damage. Some are useful to man, others less so, depending on their length, flexibility and strength and how easily they can be spun together. Malvaceae has been the most important family in this regard and includes cotton and kapok (seed fibres), and jute and kenaf (bast fibres). Bast fibres protect the phloem tubes – veins that transport sugars from the leaves to other parts of the plant. In the trunks of trees, phloem occurs just under the bark, with bast fibres providing extra strength and protection between the bark and the phloem.[14] During 'The Age of the Limes', from 6000 to 5000 BP, ancient Britons in the south depended hugely and almost exclusively on the soft and supple bast fibres of lime, mostly Small-leaved, for rope and clothing, including shoes. The importance and value of this lime continued through to the nineteenth century. During medieval times, the tree's bast fibre was so highly valued that it served as a means of payment.

Limes were also valued for their foliage – fodder for man and beast – and for their shatterproof wood, which is light,

---

14 Despite the thick bark and lime's renowned fibres, Great Spotted Woodpeckers and Treecreepers bore holes in the trunks to suck the sweet juices from the phloem tubes.

soft, even-grained and easy to carve. Little wonder that from early times, limes were coppiced to provide a regular supply of materials. Coppicing extends the life of a tree. Some Small-leaved Lime coppice stools have been estimated to be at least 6,000 years old, making it one of the oldest organisms in the British Isles.

CORNACEAE

Dogwood *Cornus sanguinea*

Landscape gardeners make much use of Dogwood to 'set their gardens ablaze' in the winter months. Dogwood is renowned for its dark red, almost purple, leaves in autumn. This strong anthocyanin pigment helps protect the living tissue by absorbing certain damaging wavelengths of light.

The pigment, which comes in various shades, also occurs in the stems when they are exposed to sunlight, particularly, of course, in the winter months. The yellows, oranges and reds of the aptly named varieties of Dogwood – 'Midwinter Fire' and 'Winter Flame' – are glorious examples of the amazing potential of anthocyanin.

Although Dogwood is part of the understory of mixed woodlands, it prefers woodland margins and often occurs in open scrub on base-rich soils, along with Spindle and Elder. It suckers enthusiastically from the roots and can often overwhelm other species in scrubland and hedgerow communities. A southern species that avoids the north and west of Britain, it returned to our isles as an understory plant around 7500 BP and expanded its range around 5000 BP in response to the early forest clearance of the Neolithic period.

Dogwood leaves (and therefore buds, of course) are arranged in opposite pairs. The leaves are simple, with distinct veins that do not reach the margin, but instead arch forward towards the tip of the leaf, like the buckthorns. The margin is entire. One well-known ID trick is to carefully snap the leaf in half at right angles to the midrib, holding the two halves very close together, and then gently draw the two halves apart. They will remain connected to each other by fragile – yet elastic – extruded strings of latex. There are no other native British trees that share this characteristic. The buds are unusual (but not unique): the tiny, primordial leaves can be seen tightly pressed and crumpled against each other, unprotected by any neat, overlapping bud scales.

The flowers are about 1cm across, creamy white and arranged in tight-forking, cymose, clusters. Note that the ovary is inferior (it lies beneath the rest of the flower). The flowers open after the leaves and do not have a pleasant scent. They are pollinated by a range of insects that feed on the accessible nectar at the base of the style; the black, two-stoned drupes ripen in October.

Dogwood

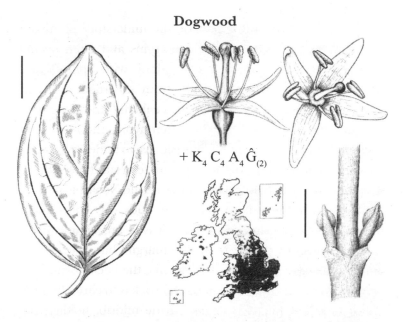

$$+ K_4 \, C_4 \, A_4 \, \hat{G}_{(2)}$$

The wood can be carved easily and was once used for making daggers, hence its old name – Dagwood. More recently it was used for butchers' skewers. For thousands of years Dogwood bark has been used as an effective anti-inflammatory. The active ingredients are the bitter and toxic iridoid glycosides, manufactured by Dogwood to deter herbivores great and small. Iridoids of the related Japanese *Cornus officinalis* in particular have played a big part in recent pharmacological research.

ERICACEAE
Strawberry Tree *Arbutus unedo*

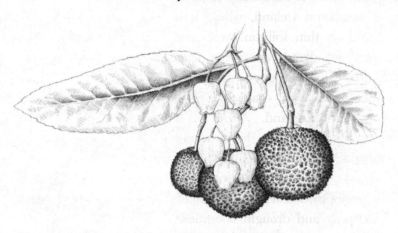

Bringing a flavour of the Mediterranean to the rugged hillsides of the Emerald Isle, Strawberry Tree, once widespread in Ireland, has become one of the rarest trees in the British Isles.

Strawberry Tree is a classic example of a tree from the semi-tropical laurisilva forests. The consistently warm and perpetually wet conditions of the tropics favour plants with evergreen foliage to take advantage of the year-round warmth and moisture, with glossy leaves to enable them to shed all those raindrops. The Strawberry Tree rode out the Ice Age in small pockets in the extreme south of Europe, particularly in the southwest, and then made its way back to Britain along the warm, wet Atlantic seaboard. It remains a mystery how it reached Ireland in 6000 BP, leaving only a trace of pollen in the southwest of mainland Britain. The first and only pollen record of this tree in Cornwall was contemporary with the first record in Ireland.

Strawberry Tree

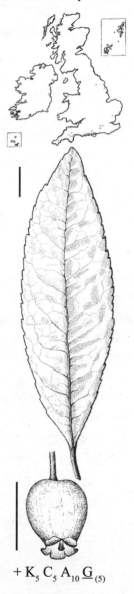

Today, Strawberry Tree occurs naturally, but rarely – only in the warm and wet valleys and hillsides of southwest Ireland, where it is found on thin soils in scrub and open woodland on rocky lake shores. It also occurs as an escape from cultivation, particularly in southwest England. Although it grows on poor soils, these are not invariably acidic, which would be typical of most other members of its family, Ericaceae. It is tolerant of salt spray and drought conditions and recovers well after fire. These attributes enable it to cope well around the Mediterranean.

The leaves are alternate, simple, evergreen and finely serrated. They are usually at least twice as long as wide, but can be much shorter and broader. The flowers are white, tinged with green or pink, and bell-shaped, like those of Bell Heather and many other members of the family. They are pollinated by bees. The red fruits that look like small strawberries (about 2cm in diameter) take a year to mature, so they are ripening on the tree when

$+ K_5 C_5 A_{10} \underline{G}_{(5)}$

the new flowers open in autumn – a double treat after most of our trees have lost their autumnal foliage. The fruit is a true berry (unlike the strawberry), with a warty skin and seeds buried inside the fruit. To my mind it has a rather dull, but not unpleasant, taste.

Strawberry Trees have a rare mycorrhizal partnership referred to as arbutoid. This is similar, but even more superior, to the highly efficient ericoid mycorrhizae of the rest of the Ericaceae, which partner with saprophytic fungi. But you'd have to be a Strawberry Tree (or an expert in the subject) to appreciate the difference!

The thick, leathery leaves of several of the laurisilva trees are equally well adapted to cope with drought and so some of them, including Strawberry Tree, became significant and attractive components of the Mediterranean maquis. Its arbutoid mycorrhizal engagement and its resilient response to fire make it a huge asset to the region. Therefore, it has understandably been recommended as a means to reclaim the impoverished soils and degraded landscapes in many locations around the Mediterranean – a much wiser choice than the highly flammable eucalypts from Australasia. Strawberry Tree may not provide as quick a return in useful timber, but the long-term ecological benefits should be regarded as a higher priority.

OLEACEAE

Wild Privet *Ligustrum vulgare*

I first became aware of Wild Privet as a child, dog walking on the North Downs, where I spent some time trying to find the source of an elusive but delicate scent – a fragrance that, ever since, I have associated with the Downs. It was of course, Wild Privet. But how very different it was from the overwhelmingly sickly smell of the introduced Garden Privet, *Ligustrum ovalifolium*, which our neighbours grew as a tightly pruned hedge on their side of our boundary while on our side it was less manicured, produced flowers and supported a Blackbird's nest.

Wild Privet was a comparative latecomer among our native trees, arriving just before we were cut off from mainland Europe by the flooding of the Channel around 5000 BP. This was too late to get across to Ireland, though it has been introduced since. It kept to the south of the country, where it grows on base-rich soils, which does not mean only the limey soils of chalk and limestone. Despite being semi-evergreen, it is not very tolerant of shade, so it is seldom found in the understory of woodlands. Instead, it prefers open habitats, which it shares with an assortment of other shrubs, such as Wayfaring Tree, Dogwood and Spindle, providing fruit and shelter for a variety of wildlife.

The creamy-white flowers of Wild Privet – with their four fused petals, two fused ovaries and two unfused stamens – are typical of the family, which also includes the heavenly-scented lilacs and jasmines. The aromatic essential oils of Jasmine in particular have long been used in perfumery. However, the most economically important member of the family is Olive, which thrives best in Mediterranean climates.

Wild Privet's winter buds are opposite and very neat, small and rounded, with more than three bud scales. The leaves are also opposite of course, and simple, about twice as long as wide, and have an entire margin. They are semi-evergreen, meaning that some, but not all, of the leaves are retained in a fully functioning state throughout the winter months, until they finally fall as the fresh leaves develop.

Wild Privet

$$+ K_{(4)} \{C_{(4)} A_2\} \underline{G}_{(2)}$$

Evergreen shrubs make good boundary hedges, and Wild Privet has been used this way since late Saxon times – some still trace the medieval boundary dykes on Romney Marsh in Kent. Today, many modern suburban gardens are fronted with the more reliably evergreen and rounder-leaved Garden Privet, introduced in 1842.

The unmistakable caterpillars of the Privet Hawk-moth, *Sphinx ligustri*, one of our largest and most striking moths, feed on privet. They also like the leaves of other Oleaceae, including Ash, which is much more common than privet. But Ash trees are sadly dwindling fast. This, in turn, will threaten the survival of the moth, which will have to rely more heavily on privet in the future.

OLEACEAE

Ash *Fraxinus excelsior*

'A tree that looks at God all day,
And lifts her leafy arms to pray'
– JOYCE KILMER (1886–1918)

This little couplet could have been written especially for the Ash tree. Particularly obvious in winter – even the down-sweeping branches rise upwards at their ends, reminiscent of an act of adoration or simply an expression of joy – Ash is an uplifting tree both in silhouette and in its ecological role as one of nature's healers.

The Ash 'keys' – single-seeded winged nutlets – are wind-dispersed, but not over great distances. Germination is reliable

Ash 'keys'

and fast and the seedlings grow quickly on the favoured soils, i.e. water-retentive and preferably limey. Ash is an opportunistic tree – a weed – but it was not an early pioneer after the Ice Age, leaving it until the slightly warmer boreal period, around 8500 BP. In certain circumstances its rapid invasion into disturbed ground can be viewed as a nuisance. But it was Ash that quickly filled the gaps left after the great storm of October 1987 and by the elms after the DED of the 1970s. Long before this, it took advantage of open spaces when Neolithic farmers started forest clearance in about 5000 BP. It healed the wounds in the forest.

By the start of the twenty-first century, Ash had become our third most widespread and abundant tree. Ash trees are light-demanding and do not, themselves, cast dense shade. This means that they permit not only a glorious carpet of spring flowers but also the germination and growth of other trees under their canopy. While most early colonisers get squeezed out by more dominant trees that follow, Ash grows tall. And despite not being ectomycorrhizal, it is able to hold its own as the new trees mature, resulting in mixed deciduous woodland, often with Ash playing a co-dominant role alongside oak or Beech, always ready to fill gaps as they occur.

The distinctive Ash twigs are pale grey and are easily recognised by their stout black buds with few bud scales.

Ash leaves are pinnately compound, with up to 6 pairs of leaflets (i.e. a total of between 9 and 13 leaflets). Two other native species have leaf shapes that may confuse: Elder, which also has opposite leaves, has only 5 to 7 leaflets, and Rowan, which has alternately arranged (not opposite) leaves and a total of 11 to 19 leaflets.

Ash

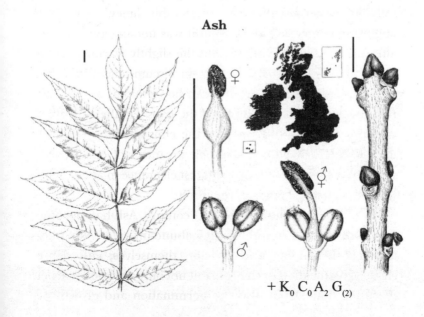

$$+ K_0\, C_0\, A_2\, G_{(2)}$$

Tree-spotting

Most Ash species, including our own, are wind-pollinated and lack petals, unlike the rest of their family, Oleaceae (see Wild Privet). Although they are petalless, the flowers are otherwise typical of the family in their hermaphrodite form, with their characteristic combination of two ovaries fused together and two stamens. Ash also produces separate male and female flowers and the proportion of these three types can vary from branch to branch, tree to tree and even from year to year. Ash celebrated gender fluidity long before humans. The flowers open before the leaves and they are self-fertile. Invariably, only one of the two ovules forms a seed, so the fruit becomes a single-seeded 'key' (a winged nutlet or samara). Copious fertile fruits are produced, as bunches of 'keys'.

Both Ash and Sycamore are opportunists that produce large numbers of wind-dispersed seeds capable of invading woodland gaps. It is not unusual to find secondary woodland dominated by these two species. Ash supports a much greater diversity of plants and animals than Sycamore, including many epiphytic mosses and lichens that cover the trunk and twigs because they prefer bark that is neither too acid nor too rough. Despite the presence of toxic chemicals (iridoid glycosides), Ash leaves support a reasonable variety of invertebrates, but these do not occur in large numbers.

Sadly, Ash is seriously threatened by the ash dieback fungus, *Hymenoscyphus fraxineus*. This fungus originated in the Far East, where it is a harmless associate with other Ash species. It was introduced to Europe in the 1970s, since which time it has destroyed nearly 80 per cent of the Ash population. Symptoms of infection were widespread in Britain by 2012. It seems most likely it was introduced by importation of infected plants or timber, despite regulations, but it could equally have arrived as spores on the wind. Fortunately, Ash trees are genetically very diverse and so some stand a chance of resisting the disease. Nevertheless, Ash represents a big proportion (12 per cent) of our tree flora, and big losses have already occurred. The ecological and visual impact in some regions will be immense.

There are two consolations. First, Sycamore is ready and waiting to fill the gaps. Though this is not ideal, it's a lot better than no trees at all and a lot quicker and cheaper than planting native species on the large scale that will be required. This could still happen – if resistant Ash specimens are identified, their 'keys' can be spread.

Second, and only for those who rely on wood stoves or wood boilers, there will be a copious supply of excellent firewood. Ash is second to none, primarily due to the high levels of oleic acid, a flammable fatty acid which enables it to burn even when green. Oleic acid occurs widely in the animal and plant kingdoms, and in particularly high concentrations in Oleaceae, notably in Olive, *Olea europaea*.

On a more sustainable note, healthy Ash is one of our most versatile of timbers. It is strong, flexible and shock-resistant, making it perfect for making robust, high-impact articles such as axe handles, hockey sticks and baseball bats. It was ideal for the original motor vehicle chassis. The Morgan Motor Company's research still maintains that the pliable Ash frame makes its cars safer on impact tests than conventional steel frames. Finally, the wood is beautifully grained – ideal for fine furniture.

AQUIFOLIACEAE

Holly *Ilex aquifolium*

'Of all the trees that are in the wood,
the holly bears the crown.'

Evocative words from 'The Holly and the Ivy', a traditional Christmas carol, early nineteenth century.

Unsurprisingly, trees feature strongly around the world as symbols in religion and mythology. For many cultures, evergreen trees are associated with the virtues of immortality and fertility. In Europe, the Druids attributed mystical powers to Holly and the Romans associated Holly with their god of agriculture, Saturn, and used it for decoration during the festival of Saturnalia. Early Christians adopted Holly from Druid, Celtic and Roman traditions, and adapted its symbolism to reflect Christian beliefs. Leafy Holly twigs, like those of many spiny shrubs, are rated as a dubious contender for the original crown of thorns, and its red berries symbolise the blood of Christ – two aspects of Christ's life more closely linked with Easter than the Nativity. Whatever your religious beliefs, Holly occupies a special place in our hearts. It also plays a unique role in the web of life. But don't they all?

Holly did not feature strongly in the British Isles until the climatic optimum of the warm, wet Atlantic period. The pollen record for 6000 BP shows an abundance of Holly in Ireland and the southwest of England. Like Strawberry Tree, Yew and Box, Holly, with its shiny evergreen leaves, is another classic example of the subtropical trees of the laurisilva forests that prevailed here before the Ice Age. Although today Holly is found throughout Britain (except in the extreme north), it is still more abundant in the milder, moister west than the more extreme temperatures of the drier east. Yet despite its requirement for a mild climate, we strongly associate Holly and Ivy with the coldest of our seasons, at Christmastime.

Holly has found a niche in the seasonal mixed oak forests. Being evergreen, it is content to thrive in the sheltered woodland understory, where it is protected from the worst of the winter and can take advantage of sunlight as the canopy cover waxes and wanes in spring and autumn. It is seldom big enough and bold enough to form a forest type of its own, but there are some mixed oak-Holly woods (I know of one in Suffolk, even) where Holly is the co-dominant.

Holly is dioecious, so only the female trees bear berries. But the flowers are misleading. Look carefully with a hand lens. Female flowers bear sterile stamens and male flowers contain sterile ovaries. The Holly berry is actually a drupe, not a berry, botanically speaking.

Holly

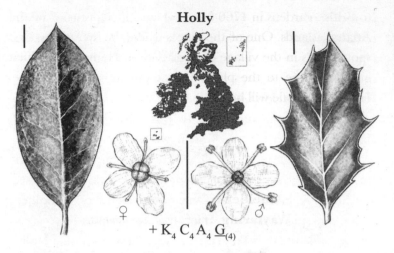

$+ K_4 C_4 A_4 \underline{G}_{(4)}$

Holly leaves are iconic for their distinctive and painful spines, but only those at browsing height are so equipped to discourage large herbivores. Those that grow above the reach of cattle have similar dimensions but an entire, unarmed margin. Both forms have a thick, waxy and glossy cuticle.

Despite the spines, Holly leaves are exceptionally nutritious, and much sought-after by large herbivores such as sheep, cattle and deer. There still exist a few small man-made Holly plantations that are regularly pollarded for winter animal fodder. Evergreen trees are generally important for wildlife – offering cover and food (leaves and fruit) in the winter. Not many invertebrates though feed on Holly foliage, but the Holly Blue butterfly, *Celastrina argiolus*, lays its eggs on the flower buds (of Ivy and Dogwood as well) and the larvae emerge in time to feed on the juices from the developing fruit.

The popular garden hybrid, *Ilex x altaclerensis*, which has larger flowers and fruit and no spines, is a naturally occurring hybrid between our Holly and *Ilex perado*, which was introduced to British gardens in 1760 from the laurisilva forests of all the Atlantic islands. One of the places where the hybrid was first spotted was in the village of Highclere in Hampshire, which gave its name to the plant. Check out its scientific name. Highclere Castle will be familiar to *Downton Abbey* fans.

VIBURNACEAE

Elder *Sambucus nigra*
Guelder-rose *Viburnum opulus*
Wayfaring Tree *Viburnum lantana*

Guelder-rose

There are three native woody species of Viburnaceae in Britain. All are large shrubs with succulent fruit and dramatically showy and scented clusters of flowers, reminiscent of wedding bouquets.

Tree-spotting

Elder occurs throughout most of Britain. It is strongly associated with fertile sites and disturbed ground, particularly where it has become nitrogen-enriched. Such sites are often associated with human settlements (historic and modern). It first flourished during Neolithic times in response to slash-and-burn farming activities. Being unpalatable to grazing animals, it is also often associated with rabbit warrens – where the ground is invariably nitrogen-enriched.

After the ice retreated, Guelder-rose was quick to migrate northwards (10,500 BP). Today, it occurs throughout Britain and as far north as the Arctic Circle, although it is scarcer in Scotland. It favours wet, neutral to alkaline soils and is found especially in thinly shaded, damp woodlands, Alder carr and wet willow thickets.

The natural distribution of Wayfaring Tree in Britain is strongly restricted to the south. It became most abundant in the pollen record once the climate was at its warmest (about 6000 BP) and after the flooding of the Irish Sea. It favours open habitats on base-rich chalk and limestone soils, and is closely associated with ancient routeways, such as the Pilgrims' Way – hence its common name. It was too late to reach Ireland.

The individual flowers of all three species are small and arranged in multi-branched cymes that look superficially like the umbel inflorescences of Cow Parsley and its allies. All species have similar flowers with fused petals and only five stamens, fused to the petals. Note that the ovary is inferior (beneath the petals). The lump in the middle is the expanded base of the three short styles. Once the ovules have been fertilised, the ovaries develop into succulent drupes.

Elder   Guelder-rose   Wayfaring Tree

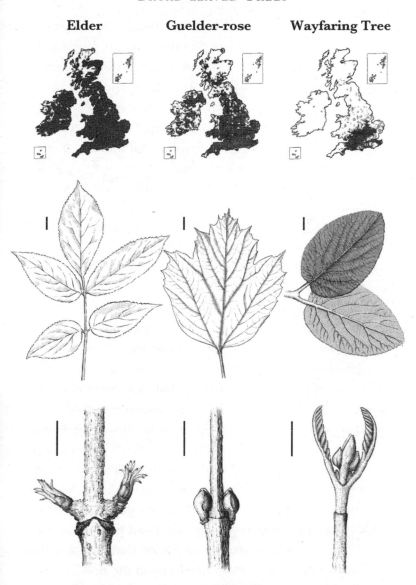

Elder

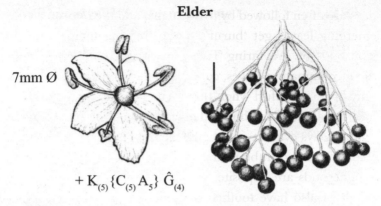

7mm Ø

$$+ K_{(5)} \{C_{(5)} A_5\} \hat{G}_{(4)}$$

Whilst considering the floral details, I am reminded that elderflowers make the best summer cordial and 'champagne', and both are brewed and drunk copiously in the Bennett household.

The common name of Guelder-rose is misleading, as the details of the flower are noticeably different from all species of Rosaceae, notably the number of stamens. Unlike Elder and Wayfaring Tree the marginal flowers of the inflorescence of Guelder-rose are distinctly larger than the rest, and sterile. Their sole purpose is to increase the attraction to pollinators of the small, fertile flowers at the centre of the inflorescence. Although they have a lovely scent, none of our Viburnaceae shrubs produce nectar. Pollinators, visiting for pollen only, are provided with a convenient platform on which to forage from flower to flower.

All three species have opposite buds, but they are distinct in other ways. Guelder-rose buds are neat and round with only two or three bud scales. Elder buds have more than three bud scales and often look tatty. This is because they tend to open prematurely on unusually warm winter days. Such days are often followed by frosty nights and the unprotected, emerging leaves get 'burnt' by the freezing temperatures. The buds of Wayfaring Tree are without bud scales, but the tiny, immature leaves, curled and folded tightly together, only begin to unfurl when the warmer spring temperatures have stabilised. Each bud is flanked by a pair of small leaves – not always evident – that give the impression of a horned Viking helmet or rabbit ears.

The buds are opposite, so the leaves must be opposite. All three also have toothed margins, but in other respects they are totally different. Wayfaring Tree has simple leaves with undersurfaces covered with stellate hairs. Use a lens to see these. (Buckthorn leaves are the closest match, but these are hairless.) The leaves of Guelder-rose are rather like the maples', lobed but lacking the heart-shaped base to the leaf blade. The leaves of Elder are pinnately compound, with 5 to 7 leaflets. The only other trees with similar leaves are Ash, whose are also opposite but have 9 to 13 leaflets, and Rowan, with 11 to 17 but arranged alternately.

Elder comes into leaf earlier than most shrubs and trees, in common with most nitrophilous species, including stinging nettles. This enables it to thrive along woodland margins, where it can take full advantage of spring and early summer sunshine. Its leaves and those of both *Viburnum* species are unpalatable to most invertebrates due to cyanogenic glycosides. When the leaf is damaged, the glycosides break down to release hydrogen cyanide, which is toxic (even to large animals, when ingested in large doses). As a result our three Viburnaceae support not only few species of leaf-eating insects but also few individuals generally, including the predators of those leaf-eaters. However, Elder's autumn leaves, like those of most nitrophilous species, are decomposed rapidly and thoroughly by just a few decomposing organisms, further increasing soil fertility.

In contrast to the foliage, elderberries are one of the most favoured and important of succulent fruits, attracting 17 different bird species – more than for any other type of native fruit. The fruit is nutritious, and easily plucked and swallowed whole. They ripen early and their popularity has a negative impact on the dispersal of other fruit-bearing species that tend to be neglected. The berries of Wayfaring Tree are eaten by thrushes until Elder is available. Guelder-rose berries become most palatable later in the winter – a valued source of energy and nutrition at a time when there is little about.

Elder supports the second greatest number of epiphytic mosses, exceeded only by Ash. It also has a distinctive lichen flora. This epiphyte richness is probably due to the fact that the soft Elder bark has one of the highest water-holding capacities of any native tree or shrub, and its bark is only moderately acidic compared with many other trees.

Elder is a rich source of dyes. The berries produce blue and purple dyes, its leaves give yellow and green, and its bark grey and black. Elder was fundamental in creating the traditional colour palette of Harris Tweed.

The Viburnaceae defence chemicals were used early in human history for medicinal purposes and are being used by pharmacologists today to derive secoiridoids, which have anti-diabetic, anti-inflammatory, immunosuppressive, neuroprotective, anticancer and anti-obesity properties – quite a repertoire!

The End ...
or Just a Beginning

YOU HAVE NOW reached the end of this guide to the 52 'native' trees of the British Isles, but I hope this will be only a beginning for you. There is so much more excitement and wonder that can follow, if you seek it. First, using the Leaf and Twig Keys to identify trees will get easier with practice, and the help of a hand lens will encourage you to spot exquisite detail that often goes unnoticed. So take the keys with you when you are on walks and keep naming the trees you meet. It's good to be on familiar terms.

Second, this approach, using keys and key features to help with identification, can be found in many larger plant guides. Now that you are familiar with the principles of the approach, you can explore other and wider fields of botany. Just looking for the right picture is a pleasurable but often unsatisfactory way of identifying plants, particularly if you are in unfamiliar country. There is so much to see and learn in the wild and in the urban landscape. Keys plus a hand lens can help enhance your knowledge and understanding.

Third, I hope that you have come to understand more about the wonder and complexity of plants. They are a few eons older than *Homo sapiens*, and the ebbs and flows of the fortunes of species and taxa tell us a lot about our world as it is now, as it has been and some insight into what it may become. Plants have found many ways to procreate, to survive in challenging climates, to compete and to cooperate. The evidence for much of this is on your doorstep and visible through a hand lens.

So – go out, introduce yourself to your neighbouring trees and wonder at their beauty, ingenuity and variety.

Useful Resources

FIELD GUIDES

MOST FIELD GUIDES provide excellent descriptions and illustrations. Those that include a comprehensive list of species may be a bit overwhelming for the beginner and generally don't have enough space to dedicate to identification keys. Some are light and fit well in a pocket, while others are best used for reference at home rather than in the field. Don't forget that trees bear flowers, so most good field guides to wild flowers will also include native trees. For our native trees, I use the following two, but they all have their merits. It is very much a matter of personal choice.

Collins Complete Guide to British Trees by Paul Sterry (HarperCollins, 2008) – illustrations are clear

Tree-spotting

Collins Wild Flower Guide 2nd Edition by David Streeter
(HarperCollins, 2016) – keys are good

Comprehensive reference sources:

Handbook of Flower Pollination, by Paul Knuth, based upon
Hermann Müller's work, translated by Ainsworth Davis
(Oxford at the Clarendon Press, Vol 1 1906, Vol II 1908,
Vol III 1909)

History of the British Flora by Sir Harry Godwin (Cambridge
University Press, second edition 1975)

The History of British Vegetation by Winifred Pennington
(Hodder & Stoughton, 1969)

Birds and Berries by Barbara and David Snow (Bloomsbury,
1988)

The Constituents of Medicinal Plants by Andrew Pengelly
(CABI, 2021)

Relevant titles in the excellent New Naturalist Library series
include:

The Natural History of Pollination by Michael Proctor, Peter Yeo
and Andrew Lack (HarperCollins, 2012)

Trees by Peter Thomas (HarperCollins, 2022)

Woodlands by Oliver Rackham (HarperCollins, 2012)

FOR ILLUSTRATIONS

Flower Fairies of the Trees by Cicely Mary Barker (Blackie and Son, 1940) – the illustrations capture the personality of each tree beautifully and each poem is a drop of wisdom about each species; Barker's books nurtured our interest (both of us) from an early age

Drawings of British Plants by Stella Ross-Craig (G. Bell & Sons Ltd., 1948) – a stunning resource with immaculate, accurate illustrations of our native plants

EASY READING

The Hidden Life of Trees by Peter Wohlleben (HarperCollins, 2015) – mycorrhizae and plant communication

The Secret Life of Trees (Penguin, 2005) by Colin Tudge – broad interest

The Treeline by Ben Rawlence (Penguin, 2022) – climate change and the future

Entangled Life by Merlin Sheldrake (Random House, 2020) – mycorrhizae and more

WEBSITES

The **British Ecological Society**'s website provides in-depth accounts about single species. It covers a wide range of topics and most of our native trees. The more recent papers are accessible online.

www.britishecologicalsociety.org/publications/journals/
journal-of-ecology/biological-flora-database

The taxonomic classification system, APG, of seed plants worldwide can be found on the **Angiosperm Phylogeny** website. It is regularly updated with changes resulting from ongoing genetic research, plus information regarding the links between evolution and taxonomy, chemistry and taxonomy, and mycorrhizae and taxonomy. But is not an easy read.

www.mobot.org/MOBOT/research/APweb/

TED TALKS AND PODCASTS

Some good presentations are delivered by Toby Kiers and Suzanne Simard on mycorrhizae and communication.

www.ted.com/talks/toby_kiers_lessons_from_fungi_on_
markets_and_economics
www.ted.com/talks/suzanne_simard_how_trees_talk_to_
each_other?language=en

David Oakes' *Trees a Crowd* is a beautifully compiled and delivered podcast. Series 3 is devoted to Britain's trees and uses a fascinating blend of science, legends and much more.
www.treesacrowd.fm

Glossary of Terms

These terms are defined as they are used in a botanical context and, particularly, as they might be employed when referring to trees.

achene	Tiny, single-seeded dry fruit that does not release its seed for dispersal – effectively, a seed with an additional protective coat; often mistakenly referred to as a seed
alien	Not native; introduced by humans intentionally or otherwise, which, in Britain, means any time after we were cut off from mainland Europe
alternate	Arranged in alternating sequence on either side of the stem; used to describe the arrangement of leaves and buds

angiosperm	A major taxonomic group ('class') that contains all flowering plants
appressed	Pressed closely against, but not joined to; used when describing buds that lie against the twig
archaeophyte	Non-native species introduced in ancient times; in Britain, this means any time before 1492
aril	A (usually) fleshy coating outside the seed coat that encloses the seed completely (Spindle) or partially (Yew)
auricle	Lobe at base of leaf blade; usually in pairs on either side of the petiole (leaf stalk)
berry	A (usually) many-seeded, succulent fruit derived from usually >1 carpel, fused together, in which the seeds do not have additional protective coats as in a drupe
biserrate	Double-toothed leaf margin, see p. 99
calyx (K)	Collective name for the sepals; occurs outside the corolla and protects the flower in bud (and sometimes the developing fruit); K in floral formulae
carpel	Basic female organ of a flower (see p. 38), composed of stigma, style and ovary (containing the ovule(s)); collectively called the gynoecium; carpel wall becomes the fruit wall

carr	Wet woodland (especially Alders and/or willows), notably on alkaline substrates
coppice	A form of woodland management used to harvest timber, wherein trees are cut close to ground level, allowed to sprout from the base and grow for 8–18 years (depending on the species) before re-coppicing
corolla (C)	Collective name for the petals in a flower that are designed to attract pollinators; C in floral formulae
crenate	Round-toothed leaf margin, see p. 99
dioecious	A species in which each tree bears male flowers or female flowers, not both; at least one tree of each sex needs to grow near enough for pollination to take place
drupe	Single-seeded, succulent fruit in which the seed is surrounded by a tough protective coat, derived, like the fleshy part, from the ovary wall
epicormic	New shoots arising from previously dormant buds growing straight from the trunk of the tree
epiphyte	An organism that grows on the bark of a tree (in Britain, typically a moss, fern or lichen)

floral formula	Shorthand summary of a flower's structure that enumerates the number of petals, stamens, etc. (see below)
glaucous	Leaves or fruit with a greyish, bluish or whitish waxy coating or bloom that usually rubs off easily
gymnosperm	A major taxonomic group largely represented by the conifers
gynoecium (G)	Female part of the flower that is composed of one or more carpels, fused together or not; becomes the fruit after fertilisation of the ovules; G in floral formulae
hypanthium	Cup-like or tubular extension of the receptacle (top of the flower stalk) surrounding the gynoecium; may develop into a fleshy false fruit after fertilisation, typical of many Rosaceae
inflorescence	Cluster of flowers, arranged in a particular pattern that is characteristic of a species, genus, or even a whole family
midrib	Main, central vein of a leaf
monoecious	A species that has separate male and female flowers occurring on the same tree
native	Occurring naturally in a location; entered British Isles before they were separated from mainland Europe by the flooding of the Channel

neophyte	Non-native; introduced by humans in recent times which, in Britain, means after 1492
nut	Large, single-seeded, dry fruit that does not release its seed for dispersal; provides nourishment to fuel germination of the seed and to act as a lure for dispersal agents
opposite	Arranged in opposite pairs on either side of the stem, each pair at right angles to those above and below; used to describe the arrangement of leaves and buds
ovule	Located within the ovary of a carpel; contains female gamete, and develops into the seed once fertilised
palmate	Lobed or divided like the fingers of a hand; used when describing leaves, e.g. maples
peduncle	Main stem of an inflorescence
petiole	Leaf stalk
pinnate	Lobes or divisions (if compound) occur in two rows on either side of the midrib; used to describe leaves, e.g. oak, Ash
pollard	Similar to coppicing but plants are cut back to a stump, at a height above the reach of browsing animals like cows or deer, rather than down to the ground

pollen	A tiny grain, produced in large numbers by the stamens; each contains one male gamete
prominent	Sticking out; used to describe buds
raceme	Type of inflorescence; stalked flowers attached spirally or in pairs along a central main stem (the peduncle)
resin	Gummy substance, typical of most conifers, containing scented volatile components; commonly exuded around wounds to combat infection
samara	Winged achene or nutlet, e.g. elm, Ash
sepal	Part of the calyx of a flower, occurring in a ring of usually five outside the petals (when present) and alternate with them; small, usually green and leaf-like
serrate	Sharp-toothed leaf margin, see p. 99
stamen (A)	Male organ of a flower; usually several stamens per flower, each composed of a filament (stalk) and an anther (sack) that produces pollen; A in floral formulae
taxonomy	Scientific classification based on evolutionary relationships

Floral Formulae

THE FLOWER OF each tree species or group of species is unique in many ways – colour, scent, size and also the number of floral parts. Flowers on their own can often be sufficient to determine a plant's identity. So it can be useful to summarise details of the flower into a shorthand or a 'floral formula'.

Working out the floral formula encourages one to explore the flower carefully and so discover another world. An example follows overleaf.

$$+ \mathbf{K}_5 \{\mathbf{C}_{(5)} \mathbf{A}_\infty\}\underline{\mathbf{G}}_{(2)}$$

+ tells us that the flower is radially symmetrical when looked at face-on

$\mathbf{K}_5$ means it has five sepals (where K = calyx)

$\mathbf{C}_{(5)}$ means it has five petals (where C = corolla) and the brackets indicate that they are fused together

$\mathbf{A}_\infty$ means it has 'an infinite number' of stamens (in practice, more than twice the number of petals)

{} these brackets explain that the stamens are attached to the petals.

$\mathbf{G}_{(2)}$ means that the gynoecium is composed of two fused carpels (count the stigmas)

$\underline{\mathbf{G}}$ the line under the G indicates that the rest of the flower is attached below the gynoecium

$\hat{\mathbf{G}}$ (not in the formula above) the hat indicates that the rest of the flower is attached to the top of the gynoecium (the gynoecium/ovary is described as being inferior in this case)

-G- (not in the formula above) the dashes on either side of the G indicate that the rest of the flower is attached to the sides of the gynoecium

v (lower case) – vestigial

Acknowledgements

THE BOTANICAL SOCIETY of Britain and Ireland (BSBI) has been extremely generous permitting us to modify their distribution maps.

The BSBI help train botanists and support recording and research projects; they publish newsletters, handbooks, local *Floras*, national distribution atlases and a scientific journal. Find out more via: www.bsbi.org

Ros would like to thank all her students, friends, family, colleagues and mentors who, over the years, have inspired and enlightened her interest in trees. Notable among these are Michael Proctor (sadly no longer with us), Peter Ashton, Alex Lockton, Hilary Marshall, Jennie Martin and David Oakes. Those who have been particularly helpful in providing guidance and suggestions for this book are Alison Foster, Brian Legg, Colin Legg, John McAllister, Hugh Robinson, David

Streeter and Peter Thomas. But it should be noted that she did not always take their advice, so they are not responsible for any remaining flaws or biased viewpoints.

Nell would like to thank Penny Legg (sadly no longer with us), Jenny Blant and Ann Evans for their immensely inspiring artistic influence.

We would both like to thank Oliver Holden-Rea of Welbeck for his endless enthusiasm and encouragement and Beth Bishop and all the staff at Welbeck for their patient and attentive support throughout.

Above all, we thank John Bennett and Niels Haenisch for keeping us inspired and for sharing their knowledge, wisdom and love.

Index